Study Skills

A Landmark School Teaching Guide

Second Edition

Joan Sedita

Landmark School, Inc.
Prides Crossing, MA

Landmark School, Inc.

Contents

Examples

Landmark School, Inc.

Preface

The first edition of the Landmark Study Skills Guide was published in 1989 and was based on Landmark School's extensive experience with study skills instruction in one-to-one tutorials, small study skills classes, and content classes. The information in the first edition has been presented to thousands of teachers and their reactions and suggestions were helpful in developing this second edition. The second edition also reflects changes made to Landmark's study skills curriculum based on the author's training and consulting experience with numerous public and private schools throughout the country. Although the Landmark School is dedicated specifically to serving the needs of students with learning disabilities, the book's approach to teaching study skills represents good, sound pedagogy which is helpful to all students.

Joan Sedita

Landmark School, Inc.

Acknowledgments

Since the publication of the first edition of the Landmark Study Skills Guide in 1989, over 8,000 educators and parents throughout the United States have ordered the book. For the second edition, I have incorporated the suggestions and feedback I received from many individuals who have been using the guide to teach study skills. I would like to thank everyone who has contributed to making this an improved edition.

I owe particular thanks to the Landmark School Outreach Program for sponsoring the publishing of this guide. In particular, I would like to thank Kathleen Hynes, the "engine" of the Outreach Program, without whom the program would not be the success it is. I also would like to thank Dan Ahearn, current director of the program, for his support of me as a writer and his dedication to the publishing of Landmark teaching material. Finally, I would like to thank Stanley Stern for the wisdom and support he has given so unselfishly to Landmark Outreach and to me personally.

Landmark School, Inc.

About the Author

Joan Sedita is a learning specialist, teacher trainer, and nationally recognized speaker on study skills and learning disabilities. Ms. Sedita worked at the Landmark School for twenty-three years as a teacher, diagnostician, study skills coordinator, upper school principal, and Director of the Outreach Teacher Training Program. She developed the study skills curriculums used at Landmark School and Landmark College, and numerous other school systems. Ms. Sedita has given hundreds of presentations and workshops for public and private schools throughout the country. She has presented at national conferences for organizations such as the Learning Disabilities Association of America, and for other educational groups such as the Principal's Center at the Harvard Graduate School of Education. She received her B.A. from Boston College, her M. Ed. from Harvard University, and currently has a private training and consulting practice in Boxford, Massachusetts.

Landmark School, Inc.

About The Landmark School Outreach Program

Established in 1977, the Landmark School Outreach Program provides professional development programs and publications that offer practical and effective strategies that help children learn. These strategies are based on Landmark's Six Teaching Principles and on over thirty years experience in the classroom. Members of the Landmark Faculty deliver graduate courses and seminars at the Landmark Outreach Center and on-site at school districts across the country. For more information about professional development opportunities and publications, visit our website at *http://www.landmarkschool.org* or contact the Landmark School Outreach Program at (978) 236–3216.

About the Landmark School

Founded in 1971, the Landmark School is recognized as an international leader in the field of language-based learning disabilities. The School is a co-educational boarding and day school with students, 7 to 20 years old, from across the United States and around the world. Within its highly structured living and learning environment, Landmark offers individualized instruction to elementary, middle and high school students. The School's program emphasizes the development of language and learning skills. Landmark students learn strategies for managing their learning differences so that they can realize their full potential both socially and academically.

Landmark School, Inc.

Landmark Teaching Principles

Imagine . . . an instructional hour in which all students are interested and involved. The teacher motivates students by making the material meaningful to them. Information is presented in a variety of interesting ways that engage the range of learning styles in the class. The teacher builds opportunities for success by presenting information in small, sequential steps, and offers positive feedback as soon as students learn and apply a relevant new skill. The teacher provides examples and clear directions for homework, and sets aside a few minutes at the end of class for students to begin the homework assignment. During this time, the teacher answers questions and makes sure each student understands the task. In short, the teacher structures the hour so each student is challenged, works at an appropriate level, and leaves the class feeling successful and confident.

The Landmark School was founded in 1971 to provide this type of structured, success-oriented instruction to students with learning disabilities. For more than thirty years, Landmark teachers have continually enhanced and refined teaching strategies to help students learn more effectively. Landmark has shared its teaching strategies with public- and private-school teachers from all over the world through Landmark seminars. All students can and do learn from Landmark's structured and success-oriented instructional models.

At the heart of Landmark's instructional strategies and programs are six teaching principles:

Provide Opportunities for Success

Providing students with opportunities for success is key. Failure and poor self-esteem often result when teachers challenge students beyond their ability. Landmark begins teaching students at their current level of ability. This approach improves basic skills and enhances confidence. As Landmark teachers introduce each new skill, they provide basic examples and assignments to build confidence and keep students from becoming overwhelmed. As the information becomes more challenging, teachers assign students easier problems to supplement the more difficult ones. In this way, those students who are having trouble with the material complete at least part of the assignment while they work at understanding and learning to apply new information. Teachers give themselves permission to provide students with whatever structure is necessary to help students be successful, such as study guides for tests, templates for writing, and guidelines for projects. Only with a solid foundation of basic skills and confidence can students make progress. That is why it is key to provide them with opportunities for success.

Use Multi-Sensory Approaches

Multi-sensory teaching is effective for all students. In general, it means presenting all information to students via three sensory modalities: visual, auditory, and tactile. Visual presentation techniques include graphic organizers for structuring writing and pictures for reinforcing instruction; auditory presentation techniques include conducting thorough discussions and reading aloud; tactile presentation techniques include manipulating blocks and creating paragraphs about objects students can hold in their hands. Overall, implementing a multi-sensory approach to teaching is not difficult; in fact, many teachers use such an approach. It is important, however, to be aware of the three sensory modes and to plan to integrate them every day.

Micro-Unit and Structure Tasks

Effective teaching involves breaking information down into its smallest units and providing clear guidelines for all assignments. This is especially important for students with learning disabilities. "Micro-uniting" and structuring are elements of directive teaching, which Landmark consistently uses with students. Micro-uniting means analyzing the parts of a task or assignment and teaching those parts one step at a time. Teachers organize information so that students can see and follow the steps clearly and sequentially. As students learn to micro-unit for themselves, they become less likely to give up on tasks that appear confusing or overwhelming. Consequently, these strategies enable students to proceed in a step-by-step, success-oriented way.

Ensure Automatization through Practice and Review

Automatization is the process of learning and assimilating a task or skill so completely that it can be consistently completed with little or no conscious attention. Repetition and review (spiraling) are critical. Sometimes students appear to understand a concept, only to forget it a day, week, or month later. It is not until students have automatized a skill that they can effectively remember and use it as a foundation for new tasks. Teachers must therefore provide ample opportunities for students to repeat and review learned material. For example, the Landmark writing process emphasizes practice and consistency. Students always brainstorm, map/outline, draft, and proofread in the same way. This provides them with an ongoing, consistent review of learned skills.

Provide Models

Providing models is simple, yet very important. It is one of the most effective teaching techniques. Models are concrete examples of what teachers expect. They do not mean that teachers are doing assignments for students. They are standards to which students can compare their own work. A model or example of a completed assignment serves as a springboard for students to begin the assignment. For example, teachers should give students a model of a sequential paragraph when teaching basic sequential paragraph writing.

Include Students in the Learning Process

Students are not passive receptacles to fill with information. They come to class with their own frames of reference. Their unique experiences and knowledge affect them as learners and should be taken into account. Therefore, during every exercise, teachers should accept student input as much as possible. They should justify assignments, accept suggestions, solicit ideas, and provide ample time for students to share ideas. Teachers should include students in assessing their own progress by reviewing test results, written reports, and educational plans. Creating and improvising opportunities to involve students in the learning process allows students to become aware of how they learn and why certain skills benefit them. As a result, students are motivated and more likely to apply those skills when working independently. In short, an included student becomes an invested student who is eager to learn.

Introduction

Why and When to Teach Study Skills

Reading, spelling, writing, and math computation are considered basic skills for learning, and acquisition of these skills is emphasized in the primary and elementary grades. For students who have difficulty acquiring these skills, remedial instruction is often available through middle and high school. Study skills are also basic skills that are essential to success in school. Too often, however, they are not addressed in school curriculums.

Most educators believe study skills are important, but too often, especially in the upper grades, teachers emphasize academic content and neglect to teach students how to learn. Teachers may assume that students learned some basic study skills in the previous grades when often they did not. Even students who have developed some of these skills continue to need advanced study skills instruction to prepare for the requirements of high school and college. When students enter middle school or high school, the academic demands increase and become more complex. Consequently, basic study skills instruction should begin when students are in the elementary grades, and continue throughout their schooling to assist them in adapting to more complex academic tasks.

A student with strong study skills will reap the benefit of these skills in all their subject areas. Students can reduce their reading time on long and difficult passages, strengthen their memories, prepare for tests, and learn to be organized. Study skills instruction teaches students how to be active learners and provides them with structured approaches to their classroom work and homework. These strategies help students avoid the anxieties and pressures that accompany academic tasks they do not know how to approach, such as taking notes from lectures or writing essays on tests. Even the best independent learners can benefit from study skills instruction by fine-tuning the strategies they have already developed.

Study Skills and Students with Learning Disabilities

How do students acquire study skills? Some students have strong problem-solving abilities that enable them to develop study skills independently. For example, there are students who are never taught note-taking skills, yet they figure out a system for taking notes from lectures once they are in high school or college. Unfortunately, many students cannot develop study strategies such as these by themselves. Students with learning disabilities in particular have learning deficits, or "weaknesses," that cause them to need direct, systematic instruction in study skills. Deficits in any of the following areas may contribute to difficulty in acquiring study skills:

- Oral and written language at the semantic (word), syntactic (sentence), and discourse (paragraph) levels

- Underlying language processing skills, such as decoding, spelling, handwriting, and reading fluency

- Reading or listening comprehension, including generalization, part-whole relationship, cause and effect, and sequencing

- Verbal or written expression, which may be evident in word-finding difficulties, limited vocabulary, and simplistic sentences and paragraphs

- Executive function skills, such as the ability to hold in mind and manipulate multiple pieces of information, and the ability to analyze information systematically

- Sustained attention

In addition, students experiencing learning difficulties due to other factors, such as English as a second language, or students who have experienced environmental, cultural, or economic disadvantage may also need study skills instruction.

Memory Issues and Study Skills

Some students have difficulty processing information because they have weaknesses in their working memory (also known as short-term memory) and/or long-term memory. We use our working memory to understand something we are hearing, reading, or seeing right now. For example, when we listen to someone give directions to a new place, we use our working memory to hold several words and sentences in mind until we have processed them. This working memory helps us find the new place. Eventually, we must move those directions into our long-term memory so we will be able to find our way again sometime in the future. Some students have difficulty with initial working memory and may also have difficulty transferring information to long-term memory.

Many of the strategies in this book are geared towards helping students become active readers and listeners as a way to augment working and long-term memory. These strategies include:

- Main idea skills: formulating main ideas in one's own words and turning main ideas into questions

- Pre-reading strategies: skimming headings and producing main idea graphic organizers, and creating pre-reading questions

- Re-stating information: summarizing and paraphrasing

- Mastery skills: revising notes and creating study guides

The Study Skills Model: A Hierarchy of Skills

The study skills model in this book presents skills in a hierarchical order in which skills build upon each other. The ability to recognize and formulate main ideas in students' own words is the most basic and important of study skills. Students need to be able to formulate main ideas at the category, paragraph, and multi-paragraph levels, in order to create a solid foundation for other skills. A basic two-column method for taking notes and a systematic strategy for generating summaries combine with main idea skills to create three "building blocks." These three skills prepare students for more advanced study skills such as textbook skills, test-preparation and test-taking skills, and research/report-writing.

Provide Direct, Systematic Instruction

Although some students are able to intuit study skills, most need explicit, direct instruction in strategies for organizing, learning, and mastering information. Teachers should emphasize to their students that it is just as important to know *how* to learn as it is to master the content. Direct, explicit instruction means teachers should talk about how and why certain study skills are applied so students can independently determine when it is appropriate to use them.

Instruction should be systematic, starting with the most basic element of a skill and progressing to more advanced elements. There is a sequence for learning and applying each study skill, and it is best to follow the sequence without skipping steps. For example, in Chapter 2, "Recognizing and Formulating Main Ideas," it is suggested that teachers follow a progression for teaching main ideas that starts with basic categorizing and advances through single paragraph and multi-paragraph levels, and finally, full text selections.

For Whom Is This Book Intended?

This book is designed for teachers working with students who have difficulty organizing themselves and their work, reading textbooks, taking good notes, and studying on a regular basis. It is also for teachers who want to include more skills instruction within their existing curriculum. It is designed as a teacher's guide, giving practical techniques and strategies, rather than as a textbook for students.

Classroom Teachers

Many classroom teachers ask, "How do I find the time to teach study skills?" This book presents teaching strategies and examples for teaching study skills that teachers can incorporate into their daily lessons. Teachers do not have to take significant time from regular classroom instruction to teach these skills, although any time that is spent will actually save time by facilitating the learning of content material and creating more effective techniques for test preparation. For example, class time spent teaching textbook highlighting at the beginning of the year will produce better results with future textbook reading assignments. Likewise, a little time at the end of each class showing students how to write assignments on an assignment page may prevent a number of time-consuming confrontations with disorganized students who tend to confuse or lose homework.

A number of schools have adopted this study skills curriculum across a team or grade level. This is an ideal situation because these skills are reinforced throughout the day by a number of teachers. The "Master Notebook System," system-wide assignment books, and two-column note-taking are the skills in this book that are most readily adaptable for use across a team, grade-level, or school.

Skills Teachers

This book will also be helpful to special education teachers, tutors, reading teachers, and others who focus specifically on skills instruction. Educators who design study skills curriculums will find the scope and sequence of the material in this guide useful for planning courses.

The more opportunity students have to learn study skills throughout the school day, the more success they will have in applying these skills. Teachers who teach study skills to students individually or in small groups should communicate with classroom teachers about ways to incorporate study skills instruction in larger classes. Students are better able to appreciate the benefit of using study skills when they see that these skills help them learn in all their classes.

Parents

The primary audience for this book is teachers, but many parents will find it helpful as well. This guide is also helpful for the growing number of parents who are choosing to home-school their children.

How to Use the Landmark Study Skills Guide

The Landmark teaching principles discussed on page xv are an important foundation for many of the techniques presented in subsequent skills chapters. These principles are frequently referenced throughout the book. In the first four chapters, the skills of organizing, recognizing and formulating main ideas, note-taking, and summarizing are presented as a continuum of skills. Once mastered, these basic skills combine to address the more complex and multi-step tasks featured in Chapters 5 through 8 (textbook, master notebook, test-taking, research and report-writing skills).

This book was developed as a teacher reference book on study skills. Because students vary in their academic abilities and previous exposure to study skills, this guide is most effective if teachers adapt it to fit the particular needs of their students. The step-by-step progression for teaching skills and the presentation of them as part of a continuum provide a framework that teachers can adapt to many different learning situations. It is the goal of this book to enable teachers to analyze a given learning situation and determine how they can best incorporate the necessary study skills instruction.

PART I

Basic Study Skills

CHAPTER 1

Organizational Skills

It is easy for teachers to assume that students possess basic organizational skills, especially once they have reached the eighth grade. Yet many students do not know what supplies they should bring to class, how to use an assignment pad, or how to estimate the time it will take to complete an assignment. Surprising as it may seem, some students do not even know how to adequately use a calendar or tell time.

Unless they are taught organizational skills, students will continue to approach their class work, homework, and test preparation in a haphazard and inefficient manner. Organizational and time-management skills are life-long skills that will benefit students into their adult years. A study conducted of college students found that planning and time management skills correlate higher with grade point averages than SAT scores. Also, strong organizational skills positively affect college achievement.[1]

The organizational skills in this chapter provide a micro-united plan of attack for schoolwork. This includes organizing notebooks and materials, using assignment pads, using calendars and schedules, and organizing study space.

Bringing the Right Materials to School

Just as a carpenter needs the right tools (such as a saw and hammer) to frame a house, students need the right tools (such as notebooks and assignment pads) to be successful at their job of learning in school. Teachers should give students and their parents a list of the materials they are expected to bring to class each day, such as notebooks, assignment pads, paper and pencils, dictionary, calendars, ruler, and calculator (see Example 1A). If possible, send the list prior to the start of the school year so students can be prepared on the first day of school. Keep a larger copy of the materials list on a bulletin board in class to use for reference. For students who are especially forgetful, provide a daily checklist for their parents to review and sign until they consistently bring in the right supplies. For many students, this structure will challenge long-standing habits and address some severe organizational weaknesses, so remember to be patient.

For teachers who work with students on limited budgets, perhaps the school PTO or other fund-raising organizations can contribute supplies for

---

Britton, B.K., and A. Tesser, 1991. Effects of Time-Management Practices on College Grades. *J. Educ. Psych.* 8 (3).

Example 1A

Materials Checklist

General Materials

❑ Notebook

❑ Pencil/Pen

❑ Paper

❑ Dictionary

❑ Calendar

❑ Assignment Pad

❑ Book Bag/Back Pack

❑ Other: _____

❑ Other: _____

Specific Materials

❑ Science

❑ Social Studies

❑ Math

❑ Spelling

❑ Language Arts

❑ Other

❑ Other

these students. In some communities, local businesses will donate out-dated notebooks and other office supplies if contacted.

Organizing Notebooks: The Landmark Master Notebook System, Phase I

Many students benefit from a standard system which is expected of every-one in the class for organizing notes, handouts, corrected tests, homework assignments, and other material that is used in school. The teacher should decide on the components of this system, teach it to the students, expect them to follow it, and emphasize its importance by including its use as part of the grading procedure. If possible, teachers who work with other teach-ers on a team should agree on the same system for all the classes they teach so students will have the system reinforced repeatedly throughout the day. Similarly, if the school principal and staff can coordinate using the same notebook system across a grade-level or throughout the entire school, the consistency will reinforce the use of the system for students and their parents, and each school year will build upon the previous year. If such systems are introduced in grades three through five and practiced in middle school, many students can independently use them by the time they enter high school.

The Landmark Master Notebook System is an ongoing system of organiz-ing, studying, and mastering material. The system has three phases:

> Phase I: Organizing Notebooks and Materials
>
> Phase II: Studying
>
> Phase III: Mastery

Chapter 6, "Study and Mastery: The Master Notebook System," reviews the studying and mastery phases of the system. Phase I, notebook organiza-tion, includes setting up the following three items.

The Working Notebook

A working notebook is one of the most important organizational tools a student can have. As its name suggests, the working notebook should con-tain all of the materials a student needs each day to complete the job of being a student. It must be brought to each class and is the place where notes are taken, and handouts or completed tests are stored. Any "live" notes (notes on material that has yet to be tested) should stay in the work-ing notebook so students can review and refer to the information in those notes while in class. Handouts should be immediately dated and placed in the notebook (teachers can initially help with this task until students can do so independently). Only information and materials that are currently relevant should be kept in the working notebook.

Any three-ring binder will serve as a working notebook, although a nylon, zippered notebook seems to hold up best. It may be a bit more expensive, but the ability to zipper-up the notebook and its contents is worth the extra cost. Also, the spine of this notebook is more flexible. The following supplies should be added to the working notebook:

- A portable, three-hole punch

- A zippered pouch with three holes to hold pencils, highlighters, pens, clips, "sticky notes," and other small supplies

- A monthly calendar

- A divider for each subject (e.g., "History"), and three to five sub-dividers for each subject section (e.g., "History Notes," "History Homework and Handouts," "History Vocabulary")

- An assignment book

These items are available at most office supply stores in a three-hole punched format so they can be inserted into the notebook. This is important because if the items are not attached in the notebook, they will get lost in backpacks or left at home or school. Schools are using more and more handouts for curriculum materials instead of textbooks, and these handouts can easily become disorganized and misplaced. The portable three-hole punch should be used to put holes in anything the student receives which does not already have holes, and this material should be inserted into the correct sub-divider as soon as it is received. It is also helpful for students to get in the habit of putting their name and date on the top of all papers.

Teachers can be flexible about the system they expect students to follow, as long as it is consistent. For most students, one large notebook for all of the subjects is generally sufficient, especially if they pull material out into a reference file on a regular basis (details on maintaining a reference file to follow). However, some students, particularly if they have a number of subjects in high school, might benefit from keeping two working notebooks: one for morning subjects and one for afternoon subjects. For younger children, the teacher may decide that several half-inch color-coordinated binders, one for each subject (e.g., blue for math, green for science, etc.) may provide a better alternative than one large notebook.

As for subject dividers, the Master Notebook System encourages the use of three to five sub-dividers for each subject. This will help students sort papers into more manageable categories. Topics for these sub-dividers are flexible. Depending on the subject, the teacher might require a separate section for notes, work sheets, vocabulary, or sample lab reports.

Monthly calendars are important to remind students and their parents of upcoming tests, long-term project due dates, and special activities. Before the beginning of each month, teachers should pass out a photocopied page of the month with these dates or direct students to copy them into their own calendars. Remind students to check these dates on a regular basis and to record the information in pencil in case dates change.

The Reserve Accordion File

If students do not routinely sort through the material in their working notebooks to remove papers which are no longer current, they will end up with mountains of material spilling out of their notebooks by the second or third month of school. The reserve accordion file is used to store notes and papers that are not currently needed in class but will be needed again for a cumulative test, a term paper, or for review. If students establish a place to store these papers in an organized way, they will be less likely to lose or throw them away and will be creating a structure to make future studying easier.

Accordion files are a good tool for reserving material. They are usually brown in color, made of flexible cardboard, and have a flap that can be closed and held in place with an attached, stretch band that wraps around the folder. A standard size for holding 8.5 by 11-inch papers is recommended, with five or six sections. Students should have one of these files for each major subject.

On a regular basis, students should review the material in the working notebook and determine which notes, homework assignments, and handouts are no longer current. They should remove these materials and assemble them into a packet, being careful to keep notes and material in the order in which they received them (dates on the top of all pages makes this task easier). The packet can be held together with a large paper clip or rubber band.

On top of the packet the student should place a cover sheet. It should include a list of main ideas from the material and a student-generated summary of the main points in the material. Example 1B is a sample cover sheet from a high school introductory biology unit. Example 1C is a sample cover sheet from a fifth grade science unit.

Example 1B

Sample Cover Sheet for Reserve File—High School Level

Biology

March 28–April 5

History of Biology

Prescientific: explaining nature through gods or supernatural

- Egyptians: Ptolemy—knowledge of biology but prescientific explanations

Scientific era: reason, natural causes, observation

- Greeks: rationalism

  - Hippocrates—father of biology

- Romans:

  - Dioscorides—father of pharmacology

  - Pliny—encyclopedia, collected knowledge

- Middle Ages: Islam added to Greek knowledge (e.g., algebra)

- Renaissance: dissection, primary observation

Summary:

Biology developed slowly over the history of mankind. In the prescientific era, people explained nature through gods or the supernatural. Although cultures such as the Egyptians had knowledge of biology and the human body, they still explained things through the supernatural. The Greeks began the scientific era of rationalism, finding natural causes through observation. Hippocrates was the father of biology, the first to look for natural causes for disease. The Romans also contributed to the development of science. Dioscorides, the father of pharmacology, categorized plants and studied how they affected the body. Pliny also advanced the cause of science by collecting knowledge the Greeks had discovered and categorizing it in the first encyclopedia. In the Middle Ages, the followers of Islam added the study of algebra to the knowledge the Greeks had already developed. Biology and the scientific method developed even further in the Renaissance through methods of primary observation such as dissection. This laid the foundation for the scientific methods we use today.

Example 1C

Sample Cover Sheet for Reserve File—Fifth Grade Level

Science

November 8–17

Electricity

Electric charges in atoms

- Kinds of electric charges in an atom
- How atoms become charged

Charged objects

- How charged objects affect each other
- How a charged object loses its charge

Moving electrons

- Materials that carry electric currents
- What is an electric circuit?
- Using electricity safely

Summary:

Electricity comes from positive and negative charges found in atoms. Losing or gaining electrons can charge atoms. Objects can become negatively or positively charged if they lose or gain electrons. This can happen when objects are rubbed against each other. Objects that have the same charge repel each other, and objects with opposite charges are attracted to each other. An electric discharge happens when an object loses its charge. When positive or negative electrons leave the object it may cause a spark. When electrons continuously move they become electric current. Some materials (like metal) are conductors and they help electric current run. Other materials (like rubber) are insulators and they stop electric current. The path of an electric current is called an electric circuit. Electrons move along an electric circuit. There are several things you can do to handle electricity safely. For example, never touch an appliance if you are wet, and stay away from electric power lines.

For students in the elementary grades or those who are just learning how to keep a reference file, the teacher may need to develop the cover sheet and give it to the class. Once students are able to develop sufficient main idea and summarizing skills on their own, they can create the cover sheet by themselves. Creating a cover sheet as a class provides a good review strategy and opportunity to model the thought process and steps involved. Following class discussion, the teacher can write the information on the board for the class to copy. A concise list of new vocabulary and definitions may also be added to the cover sheet.

Once the packet has been assembled and a cover sheet attached, the packet should be placed in the first divider of the accordion file. This packet becomes a study guide that can be used to prepare for the unit test, or later for a semester test. At the end of the next chapter, a second packet should be placed in the second divider of the file. After several weeks of study, the accordion file will contain several study packets that neatly divide the material for a course into manageable study units.

Ultimately, the goal is for students to transfer material from the working notebook to the reserve file independently and to keep the reserve file at home. Until this skill has been mastered, however, teachers may want to store the reserve files in the classroom. An alternative to using accordion files is to keep reserve packets in hanging folders in a filing cabinet.

Teachers should take time at the beginning of the school year to teach students how to use the working notebook and reserve accordion file. After the initial setup, provide time in class for students to organize, punch holes, and store materials whenever papers are distributed. Some students may need individual help from a teacher's aide or may need to be paired up with another student who is able to assist them.

Each student should have a "notebook checklist" (see Example 1D). The teacher, the student, another student partner, or a parent can refer to this list to check off the items that are required for each student's notebook. Teachers can choose to grade this or give a small reward if a student successfully completes notebook checks.

Initially, the teacher should set aside a regularly scheduled time in class for students to move papers into the reserve file. Some teachers prefer to do this on the same day (e.g., every Friday morning) or at the end of each chapter or unit of study. It is important to go no longer than three weeks between opportunities for moving papers. Depending on the age and ability of the students, as well as their experience with this system in previous grades, their ability to maintain the working notebook and reserve file on their own will improve during the school year.

Example 1D

Notebook Checklist

Item	Possible Points	Your Points
Three-hole punch	5	___
Zippered pouch with all ingredients	15	___

- pens and pencils
- correction fluid
- paper clips
- highlighters
- calculator

Monthly calendar with dates	10	___
Subject dividers	5	___
Sub-dividers for each subject	10	___
Items in reference section	15	___

- spelling list
- transitional word list
- personal schedule
- book report template
- "How to Answer an Essay Question"

All papers are dated	10	___
All papers are filed correctly in sections	20	___
Overall neatness of notebook	10	___

TOTAL POSSIBLE POINTS   100   YOUR POINTS ___

It is important that students are able not only to organize the material in the working notebook and pull papers out into the reserve file, but also that they understand the reason for organizing and maintaining the notebook in this way. If students know and can verbalize the rationale, they will be able to check their own progress and will be more likely to use it independently in other classes or academic situations.

Reference Section

The third item in the organizational phase of the Master Notebook System is the reference section. This is a collection of resources that students need to reference quickly in class. It can be kept in a smaller, three-ring binder or in a section at the back of the working notebook. The reference section may include:

- A spelling list of commonly misspelled words (this list may change on a weekly or monthly basis)

- A list of transitional words and phrases that will improve the quality of writing assignments (see Example 1E)

- Math facts

- Charts or graphs, such as a time line of events for social studies

- Directions such as "How to Answer an Essay Question" (see Chapter 7, "Test Preparation and Test-Taking Skills" on page 101)

- Templates for special assignments, such as a book report or science lab

Initially, teachers should determine what goes into the reference section, but gradually students can be encouraged to add their own individualized items (e.g., a schedule of music lessons). Plastic sheet protectors with three-ring holes are an excellent way to ensure that the pages in the reference section are easy to find and do not rip out.

Organizing Homework Assignments

Requiring the same assignment book for everyone in the class, teaching students how to use it, and checking it on a regular basis will create a significant improvement in the efficiency, timeliness, and quality of homework. There are a number of companies that sell various styles of assignment books and agenda mates. Often these companies market directly to schools, and some will even print the school's logo and school rules at the beginning of the

Example 1E

Transitional Words and Phrases

Purpose	Words and Phrases
To add information or continue a line of thought	and, too, also, in addition, again, further, besides, furthermore, likewise, moreover, another, equally important, similarly, in the same way
To limit, contradict or contrast an idea	but, yet, however, still, on the contrary, although, nevertheless, otherwise, at the same time, on the other hand
To stress a point	above all, even more, in other words, that is, in fact, in short, most important
To illustrate a point	for example, for instance, as you will see, to illustrate
To show cause/effect or results	therefore, thus, as a result, consequently, for this reason, because, accordingly, hence, as you can see
To list, to present a series	first, second, third, then, next, after that, lastly, finally, in addition, also
To indicate time order	before, after, since, while, then, later, finally, in the meantime, now, at this time, during, presently, eventually, gradually, sooner or later, at length
To indicate spatial order	here, there, beyond, farther on, to the left/ right, over, between, beside, nearby, below, adjacent to, opposite to, parallel with
To summarize or conclude	therefore, thus, consequently, in conclusion, in other words, in summary, in brief, to sum up, to conclude, hence

books. The large chain stores for office supplies also carry a variety of student assignment books, particularly at the start of the school year. Many of these products are well designed and their distribution to everyone in the school reinforces consistent use of assignment books. Teachers may find, however, that the teaching team or school would prefer to design its own assignment book that is tailored to the needs of the students. A local printer can print and bind them, and perhaps the local business community would be willing to contribute to their cost and printing. Either way, be sure the assignment book includes the following essential ingredients:

- Three-holes so it can be kept in the working notebook
- A sturdy cover and binding to last for the school year
- Plenty of room to write detailed homework descriptions for each subject (preferably one page per day)
- A space for a daily, parent/teacher comment or signature

In addition, consider the following optional ingredients:

- A column to note the time it takes to complete each assignment, both estimated and actual
- A checkbox to be marked when an assignment is completed
- A "long-term" column to plan for assignments which are not necessarily due the next day

Example 1F provides a template for a daily assignment sheet that incorporates these suggestions.

Teachers should provide time during class when students copy homework assignments into their books. It is tempting when class time is running out to call out an assignment as students are getting up to leave, but this makes it difficult for those students who have weak organizational or direction-following abilities to be successful. Assign homework early in the class period so students can record it accurately and ask questions. Include the purpose of the assignment, the due date, the steps and guidelines for completing the assignment, what should go home (e.g., textbook), and a rough estimate of how long it must be, or how much time it might take to complete. Choose one area of the blackboard where homework will always be written or use a large newsprint pad on a flip chart. Each page can be flipped over for the next day's assignment, and teachers or students can easily flip through previous pages to check on back homework assignments. This is helpful when students miss class.

Example 1F

Daily Assignment Sheet

Date _____

English/Lang. Arts   Time to Complete: Estimated _____ Actual _____ Due Date _____

____ I have completed the assignment   ____ There was no homework

---

Math   Time to Complete: Estimated _____ Actual _____ Due Date _____

____ I have completed the assignment   ____ There was no homework

---

Science   Time to Complete: Estimated _____ Actual _____ Due Date _____

____ I have completed the assignment   ____ There was no homework

---

Social Studies   Time to Complete: Estimated _____ Actual _____ Due Date _____

____ I have completed the assignment   ____ There was no homework

---

Other   Time to Complete: Estimated _____ Actual _____ Due Date _____

____ I have completed the assignment   ____ There was no homework

---

LONG-TERM ASSIGNMENTS/TESTS

PARENT/TEACHER COMMENTS:

Signatures _____   _____

Given the number of tasks a teacher is expected to complete in any given day, it is common to feel that there is not enough time to teach and practice the notebook and organizational skills detailed in this chapter. However, many teachers have incorporated these suggestions and have found that the time it takes at the beginning of a school year to develop these skills is made up as the year progresses and as students are completing homework more efficiently.

Some students do not complete homework even when they have written it clearly in the assignment book and are capable of doing the work. In these cases, if parents are supportive, teachers should work out a system for parents to check work and sign off at the bottom of the assignment book. If the directions are detailed and specific, it will be easier for parents to determine if the assignment has been completed.

Students often find it difficult to estimate how long an assignment or several assignments will take to complete. They start their homework by taking out the first book they find and keep on working until they are too tired, their favorite TV show comes on, or their parents tell them it is time to go to bed. They often stop before their work is completed and then scramble to finish homework the next day between classes or during lunch. Some students waste time because they do not know where to begin or are overwhelmed by having several assignments at once. Homework is more manageable and less threatening if students learn to micro-unit the work. In class, students should estimate how much time they should spend on each assignment and then note how much time it actually took to complete each one (see Example 1F). Teachers should remind students to count only the time they spend on homework and not the time taking bathroom or snack-breaks, or sharpening pencils.

Teachers can also suggest that students organize their homework by planning the order in which they will complete subjects. Doing the more difficult assignments first, before they become tired, is usually the best approach. If students have a study hall or other time during the school day that they can work on homework, show them how to pick one or two short assignments that they know they can complete in that time.

Example 1F includes a space at the bottom of the day's assignments to keep track of upcoming tests and long-term assignments (such as book reports). Teachers should help students determine what they should be doing on a daily basis to study or complete assignments by the due date. Also, they should encourage students to note on the assignment page any special tasks (such as stopping by the library to pick up a book) or personal commitments. This will allow them to make connections between school and personal time.

Organizing Time

In addition to organizing their materials, students must learn to organize their time on a long-range and short-range basis. The best tool for long-range planning is a monthly calendar. Teachers can prepare students by placing a semester or school year calendar on a wall or bulletin board where it will be convenient and easy to see. Fill in all holidays, vacation days, and other special activities on the class calendar and always refer to it when discussing due dates or announcing a quiz or test. Have students copy this information into the calendars in their Master Notebooks.

While long-range planning organizes the student's time in terms of long-term due dates and broad events, short-range planning is needed for daily specifics. A personal weekly/daily plan book is best. Many adults will admit that without their daily planners their lives would be a mess, so why shouldn't teachers show students how to use these useful tools? A daily calendar should not be used to list homework assignments; it is a separate tool for keeping track of time. Instead of a calendar book, students can use a daily planning page that the teacher distributes and the students place in their Master Notebook. If the school is printing its own assignment books, calendar pages can be included (see Example 1G for a sample daily planning page).

At the beginning of each week, teachers should share the goals for daily lessons and announce any quizzes or tests. Students should take out their calendars at this time and note the information. If the opportunity arises to work individually with students, teachers can show them how to leave time for other things, such as sports or family obligations, as they plan daily activities. Demonstrate how to set aside some weekend time to study for a test, use the library, or do weekly reviews.

It is often difficult for parents to help their children determine when to do homework and other activities that are important at home (such as chores). A homework routine that is scheduled and consistent works best. Example 1H is a daily time sheet to be used to plan all of the activities that are important to parents and the student. It can be a useful tool when determining if a student will have enough time to join an after-school club or take on the practices required by sports teams.

Setting a consistent finish time can be as important as establishing a regular time to begin homework. If a homework period is open ended, students may hurry their work. Teachers and parents should let students know that if they are done before finish time, they will read or write in a journal until the homework period is over. Setting a finish time discourages rushing and encourages students to complete the work to the best of their ability.

Example 1G

Daily Planning Page for School

Today's Schedule:

8:00–9:00 _____   4:00–5:00 _____

9:00–10:00 _____   5:00–6:00 _____

10:00–11:00 _____   6:00–7:00 _____

11:00–12:00 _____   7:00–8:00 _____

12:00–1:00 _____   8:00–9:00 _____

1:00–2:00 _____   9:00–10:00 _____

2:00–3:00 _____   10:00–11:00 _____

3:00–4:00 _____

Example 1H

```
┌─────────────────────────────────────────────────────────────────────┐
│                                                                       │
│                  Daily Planning Page for Home                         │
│                                                                       │
│                                                                       │
│   Date: _____                                     │
│                                                                       │
│                                                                       │
│                                                                       │
│   3:00 _____        6:30 _____        │
│                                                                       │
│                                                                       │
│   3:15 _____        6:45 _____        │
│                                                                       │
│                                                                       │
│   3:30 _____        7:00 _____        │
│                                                                       │
│                                                                       │
│   3:45 _____        7:15 _____        │
│                                                                       │
│                                                                       │
│   4:00 _____        7:30 _____        │
│                                                                       │
│                                                                       │
│   4:15 _____        7:45 _____        │
│                                                                       │
│                                                                       │
│   4:30_____         8:00 _____        │
│                                                                       │
│                                                                       │
│   4:45 _____        8:15 _____        │
│                                                                       │
│                                                                       │
│   5:00 _____        8:30 _____        │
│                                                                       │
│                                                                       │
│   5:15 _____        8:45 _____        │
│                                                                       │
│                                                                       │
│   5:30 _____        9:00 _____        │
│                                                                       │
│                                                                       │
│   5:45 _____        9:15 _____        │
│                                                                       │
│                                                                       │
│   6:00 _____        9:30 _____        │
│                                                                       │
│                                                                       │
│   6:15 _____        9:45 _____        │
│                                                                       │
└─────────────────────────────────────────────────────────────────────┘
```

Organizing Study Space

Where students study and do homework is almost as important as how they study, especially for students who are easily distracted. Teachers should consider offering the following suggestions to students and their parents regarding their at-home study space. It should include:

- A good light

- A comfortable yet supportive chair

- A clear work space free of visual distractions (such as posters or toys) and auditory distractions (such as TV, radio, conversations, or the sound of other children playing)

- A regular place where the student always studies and, if possible, uses only for studying

- All necessary tools and supplies, such as a pencil sharpener, ruler, paper, calculator, and dictionary

Depending on how long they are working, students should plan to take appropriate breaks to avoid becoming fatigued. They should complete one assignment at a time; all other work should be removed from the work surface so they do not become distracted or feel overwhelmed by the other assignments they have yet to complete.

In addition, students should identify one place in the home where they can assemble everything they will need for the next day of school. This "arrival and departing station" can be a corner on the floor near the front door, a corner of the dining room table, or perhaps a shelf near the kitchen door. When they are finished with homework, it is a good time to assemble their work, books, and any special items they might need for the next day (e.g., gym suit, show-and-tell item) and place them in this spot. Things should be ready to walk out the door on time.

Not all parents are able to help their children set up and maintain a good study place, and it sometimes frustrates teachers when they have no way to monitor what happens at home. At the very least, however, teachers can encourage students to think about setting up a good home space by practicing in the classroom. When students are working in class, require that they clear the desk of all material except for their current assignment. Remove as many distractions as possible and take planned breaks. Model and discuss good work habits in class so students can emulate them at home.

Organizing the Classroom

Setting a good example and modeling organizational skills for students goes a long way toward helping them see the importance of being organized. Some suggestions:

"How-To" Lists
Place posters on the walls with lists of helpful items, check lists, and directions to follow. Some examples include:

- A list of transitional words

- Items needed for the Master Notebook System

- The three strategies for finding a main idea (see Chapter 2)

- Proofreading steps (capitalization and punctuation, spelling, content, and sentence and paragraph structure)

- Directions for how to take two-column notes

- Common abbreviations

Visual Reminders versus Visual Distractions
Everyone enjoys colorful posters and samples of student work on bulletin boards and walls. However, too much information can be distracting and overwhelming, and interfere with some students' ability to focus on well-chosen posters and lists of study and organizational strategies. Moderation is key to using visual reminders on classroom walls. Teachers should update the information regularly, keeping the items that will help throughout the year and rotating material that is temporary. Teachers should confine temporary material to one area of the classroom.

Supply Bank
Students inevitably lose materials, sometimes even their Master Notebooks. Teachers should create a bank of supplies (pencils, paper, extra notebooks, section dividers, highlighters, etc.) so replacement will be easy. Teachers can cover the cost of these items by asking parents to set up a five-or ten-dollar "bank" which students can draw against. Teachers can also send home a charge slip. If all the teachers in one grade or school have adopted a similar Master Notebook System, the student council might con-

sider coordinating a supply bank and selling materials during lunch or recess.

If students are on a limited budget, the school-supply budget or P.T.O. may cover the cost of these items. In some communities, there are businesses that are willing to donate notebooks and other office supplies they no longer need.

Setting Clear Expectations

Students are better organized when they know exactly what is required. When teachers are clear about expectations for materials (notebooks, calendars, and supplies), for classroom behavior, and for performance on specific tasks, students can plan accordingly.

It is important for teachers to share the schedule for the week with students and to make sure they understand expectations for homework before they leave the room. Be equally clear about expectations for class behavior. Communicate the policy for requests such as being excused during class. When must students raise their hand, and when is it all right to speak out? What is the policy for missed homework or tests? Post a list of basic classroom rules for student reference and then stick to those rules.

Teachers should clarify expectations each time a new assignment is introduced. Some students do not know how long a writing assignment should be and may hand in too little or too much. Give examples and models, or suggest how much time an assignment should take. Before giving a test, describe what the questions will be like. Will it be objective, essay, or both? How much time will they have? Can they use their books or notes? Don't assume students know what is expected. Encourage them to ask questions when they are unclear about what they should do. Call on students to reverbalize directions as a way of checking that they have listened and understood.

Recognizing and Formulating Main Ideas

The ability to recognize and formulate main ideas is the most important of the study skills. It lays the foundation for note-taking, summarizing and paraphrasing, textbook skills, test preparation and study, and research and report-writing. When students process information using main ideas, they are better able to organize, comprehend, remember, and express that information. Thinking in terms of main ideas is like having a key that unlocks the system for processing information. Students who do not recognize and formulate main ideas tend to get lost in the details or become overwhelmed with too much information.

Main idea skills are also essential to good writing. Students cannot construct good paragraphs unless they know how to group detail sentences into single paragraphs with main ideas. They cannot organize their thoughts into a composition or answer an essay question unless they can group their ideas into main idea categories. The ability to develop outlines and other graphic organizers before writing is rooted in the ability to determine main ideas.

Thinking in terms of main ideas is a useful skill in everyday life, and it is helpful for teachers to introduce the concept of main idea by providing examples of things around us that are organized this way. For example, items in the supermarket can be found in certain areas of the store, such as the dairy, produce, or bakery, and the food aisles are stacked with like items such as cereal or canned vegetables. The large signs on the walls of the store and the lists at the front of each aisle serve to remind customers of the location of items they need.

On a smaller scale, most people organize their clothes in a dresser by grouping like-items: socks and underwear in one drawer, shirts in another, pants in another. Kitchen items are usually grouped into cabinets by category: glasses and plates, canned goods, and pots and pans. Similarly, information on newscasts is presented by category: national news, local news, sports, and weather. Many radio and television stations even assign a different anchor for each segment of the news. Teachers should point out to students that just as information and things in daily life are organized by main ideas, information from lectures, books, and library research can also be organized by main ideas.

A main idea can be the category for a list of items, the topic of a paragraph, the theme of an essay or lecture, the topic of a textbook chapter, or the thesis of a term paper. The process for determining a main idea is the same whether a student is categorizing a simple list of items or identifying main themes in a college essay. Students should follow these three steps:

- Identify the details

- Compare the details to determine what they have in common

- Use your own words to create a statement about what they have in common (the main idea)

This process should be introduced to students in the first grade, and reinforced and developed in each successive grade as reading and lecture material becomes longer and more complex.

When categorizing a list of words, the words become the details. These are compared in order to determine the common category, which then becomes the main idea. When reading a paragraph, the sentences become the details, and these must be compared in order to determine the main idea. In most paragraphs the main idea is already stated as a topic sentence. However, many paragraphs do not have a topic sentence, and the main idea must be inferred and stated in the reader's own words.

For multi-paragraph material, there will be a hierarchy of main ideas. For example, in a reading selection with four to eight paragraphs, the main ideas from all the paragraphs are compared to determine the main idea of the whole selection. For lengthier selections of several pages or more, the main ideas from all the paragraphs are compared to develop section main ideas, and then the section ideas are compared to determine the main idea of the whole selection. Many textbooks provide headings and sub-headings (usually highlighted in bold print) which can help identify section main ideas. However, some lengthy material does not include bold headings, and students must infer the entire hierarchy of main ideas and state it in their own words.

Teaching Main Idea Skills

It is important to introduce the concept of main idea by using structured examples. Eventually students will learn to formulate main ideas from all types of reading and listening sources, some of which may be disorganized or poorly written. Initially, however, students should use organized material to develop and practice the ability to discern main ideas and put them in their own words. Teachers should follow this progression to introduce and teach main idea skills:

1. Categorize and find the main idea for lists of words.

2. Identify main ideas in paragraphs with topic sentences.

3. Infer and formulate main ideas in paragraphs without topic sentences.

4. Identify the main ideas in paragraphs and the overall main idea of multi-paragraph selections.

5. Identify the paragraph, section, and overall main ideas of lengthier selections.

6. Practice main idea skills at the categorizing, paragraph, and multi-paragraph levels using a variety of sources (e.g., material from science, social studies, and literature).

Categorizing Main Ideas

The purpose of categorizing is to demonstrate that people, places, things, and ideas can be grouped together into main ideas. Teachers should introduce categorizing by listing similar items and asking students what they have in common. For example:

Fruit is the category (main idea) for apple, orange, and banana

Emotions is the category (main idea) for anger, love, and sadness

For younger students and students having difficulty generating the category in their own words, include the category in the list of details. For example:

Brown, Orange, **Colors**, Yellow, Blue, Green

Teachers can provide further practice by instructing students to separate the details into two related main idea categories. For example:

List: Roosevelt, Hitler, Stalin, Mussolini, Tojo, Churchill

Category 1: Leaders of the Allied countries in World War II (Roosevelt, Stalin, and Churchill)

Category 2: Leaders of the Axis countries in World War II (Hitler, Mussolini, and Tojo)

Although there are specific workbooks available for practicing categorizing skills, most content material used in regular classes offers plenty of opportunities to categorize. Students will see more value in learning this skill if it is related to information they are already studying. Some examples by subject:

Science:

Plant or animal species

Types of weather, cloud formations

Lists of elements in physics

Parts of the human cell

Social Studies:

Countries or states by geographic region

Customs from different cultures

Grouping similar events

English:

Parts of speech

Sentence types

Vocabulary

Characters in literature

Math:

Types of measurement

Types of word problems

Algebraic formulas

Geometric shapes

Main Ideas in Paragraphs

The next step in the progression of developing main idea skills is to recognize main ideas at the paragraph level. Once students can identify main ideas in paragraphs and state the ideas in their own words, they are better able to understand, organize, and remember most reading material. A paragraph is the most basic unit of discourse and is usually constructed around a single main idea. The comprehension of lengthy reading selections requires the ability to micro-unit those selections into paragraphs with main ideas. Another common term for describing paragraph main ideas is "chunking." Chunking means grouping together detail sentences, which share a main idea.

Teachers should introduce this skill by using well-structured paragraphs with a topic sentence that clearly states the main idea and detail sentences that clearly support that main idea. Although the first sentence of a paragraph usually contains the topic, teachers should use some paragraphs in which the main idea sentence is located in the middle or at the end. This will teach students that the first sentence does not always contain the main idea.

Next, students should practice formulating the main ideas of paragraphs that do not contain a topic sentence. Instead, the main idea must be inferred. The transition from identifying stated main ideas to formulating implied main ideas is difficult for many students, so teachers should be sure to provide plenty of practice with this skill.

Teachers do not need to prepare material to practice these skills. Paragraphs from textbooks, reference books, or other material used in content classes often contain structured paragraphs, which can be used to practice identifying and formulating main ideas. The one-paragraph news summaries found in most newspapers are also a good resource for practicing these skills. Teachers should remove the headline and instruct students to compare the detail sentences in the paragraph and determine what they have in common as a way to determine their own main idea title (see Example 2A).

Example 2A

Sample News Summaries

Heart Disease Still No. 1

Heart disease remains the nation's largest killer, taking a life every 32 seconds. But researchers in Monterey, California have made unbelievable progress in taming the disease, according to the American Heart Association. Studies released Sunday show that deaths from heart and blood vessel disease have dropped 24 percent during the past decade. Researchers attribute the improvement to healthier living habits and better treatment.

Reprinted with permission of The Associated Press.

Land Offer Nets Big Response

An offer in Minneapolis of free 40-acre parcels for people willing to settle in a remote county on the Canadian border has brought more than 4,000 inquiries, some from as far afield as West Germany and Guam. Homesteaders will be required to build a home and live there for at least 10 years. They are expected to be self-sufficient, so they do not drain the local economy.

Reprinted with permission of The Associated Press.

Workbooks are available which contain exercises for finding the main idea. In these, students are directed to select the main idea from a list of choices. With this type of practice material, teachers should remove the main idea choices to make the task more realistic. Real-life reading assignments do not provide a list of choices after each paragraph.

Main Ideas in Multi-Paragraph Selections

Once students are capable of identifying and formulating main ideas in paragraphs, they can begin identifying a hierarchy of main ideas from multi-paragraph selections.

Initially, the teacher should use fairly structured selections, from three to eight paragraphs in length, which have one main idea per paragraph. Students can determine the main ideas paragraph-by-paragraph and list these on paper. Next, they should compare the main ideas to determine what they have in common. This becomes the section main idea. If they are using a selection from a textbook chapter, the section main idea may already be highlighted in bold print at the beginning of the selection. Using the first three paragraphs from the introduction of this book as an example, the main ideas would be:

Paragraph 1: Unlike reading or writing, study skills are often not taught in school.

Paragraph 2: Study skills should be taught in all grades.

Paragraph 3: Study skills instruction will help all students become better learners.

The section main idea is **"Why and when to teach study skills,"** which is also the heading above the paragraphs.

Example 2B is a four-paragraph selection, which has one main idea per paragraph:

Paragraph 1: Juvenile offenders are sentenced by juvenile juries in Denver.

Paragraph 2: Juvenile juries are popular.

Paragraph 3: These juries give sensitive, imaginative, and effective judgements.

Paragraph 4: There are several reasons why the jury program is a success.

The section main idea is **"A juvenile jury system is working well in Denver."**

Example 2B

"Juvenile Juries—Peer Pressure at Work"

On the theory that it takes a teen-ager to know a teen-ager, juvenile juries in Denver are deciding the sentences given to some first-time offenders at the junior and senior high school level. The student jurors, volunteers all, pass sentence only on young people who have admitted guilt and signed contracts with the district attorney's office agreeing to abide by whatever penalty their peers impose. The juries handle such crimes as assault, possession of dangerous weapons or marijuana—all but the most serious. Typical sentences include unpaid community service, obeying tight curfews, avoiding the city's high-crime Capital Hill area, attending school, getting a job or making full restitution in cases of theft or vandalism.

Given the choice, virtually all delinquents opt for sentencing by the youthful juries. "It's a lot better than going before a judge," says a 16-year-old who stole a car at knifepoint and was required to accept counseling and strict curfew rules for a year. "It was good to talk to someone who understands," he says of his jury.

The volunteer juries have turned out to be sensitive and imaginative. They have handed out some less-than-draconian but effective decrees: ordering a 17 year old to join an athletic team; rebuking a father for belittling his son and "being part of the problem," instructing a youth to write a letter of apology to a policeman. Says Zoralee Steinberg, who heads Denver County's "diversion" (i.e., from the criminal justice system) program for young offenders, "The insight these kids have is amazing."

Denver County District Attorney, Dale Tooley, who with Steinberg presented the jury program to the students last spring, believes one reason for its success is that the kids get a hearing within days after their arrest, instead of brooding for two or three months while awaiting a conventional trial. More important perhaps is the program's philosophy that young people are responsible for their actions, coupled with close follow-up; the district attorney's office remembers delinquents on holidays and birthdays—even after they have left the program—to make sure that they observe whatever curfew is set. So far, only one of the 55 offenders sentenced by juvenile juries has been charged with another crime.

Here is one technique for developing independent application of main idea skills in multi-paragraph material:

1. The teacher creates a main idea list from paragraphs in a selection.

2. The students read the selection and review the main idea list.

3. The teacher discusses with the students which sentences in the paragraphs contribute to the main ideas and which are supporting details.

Once students practice this, the teacher can distribute partially completed main idea lists, and the students fill in the missing main ideas. This technique is useful when the students in the class differ in their ability to identify and formulate main ideas. Students who have mastered main idea skills can be asked to generate all of the main ideas. Students who are adept at finding main ideas in paragraphs with topic sentences, but still need practice inferring main ideas, can work on a partially completed list. And, students who cannot find main ideas at all can practice on a completed list. This is a simple accommodation, which enables students at different ability levels to use the same reading selections.

Students should practice formulating main ideas from a variety of sources so they can become proficient at applying the skill in all their classes. For example, science material is often presented differently than social studies material. Teachers should use other sources as well as, such as newspapers, magazines, reference material, and primary sources such as diaries and letters, that have writing styles that differ from that typically used in textbooks.

Unfortunately, many writers, including textbook authors, do not always write paragraphs containing single, identifiable main ideas. Also, literary materials such as poems or short stories are structured so that a single main idea per paragraph is not always possible. For example, the main ideas in Example 2C are difficult to determine because the story contains numerous quotations. Making the transition to recognizing main ideas in less structured material is difficult for many students and requires a lot of practice.

Techniques for Finding the Main Idea

"Goldilocks"

There are several strategies that can be used to determine the main idea and how it should be stated. The first is the "Goldilocks Technique." In the children's story "Goldilocks and the Three Bears," Goldilocks finds that when she sits on the bears' beds, one is too hard, one is too soft, and one is just right. When she tastes the bear soup, one is too hot, one is too cold, and one is just right. Similarly, when students state a main idea, sometimes they are too general, sometimes they are too specific, but we want them to be just right. Students should ask themselves these questions as they formulate main ideas:

- Is my main idea too specific?

- Is my main idea too general?

Refer to the first sample news paragraph in Example 2A:

- **Main idea that is too specific:** "Heart disease takes a life every 32 seconds."

Example 2C

"The Christmas I'll Never Forget"
By Richard Pritchett

On Christmas Eve for more than a quarter of a century now, John M. Horan, the postmaster in Stow, Massachusetts, has placed two refrigerator shelves beneath the family tree in the living room of his home.

They are ordinary shelves similar to those you will find in most refrigerators manufactured back in the forties and fifties. Yet Horan, who is 50, has preserved them carefully, guarded them from rust, and will always place them under the family tree on the great day.

On December 18, 1955, paratrooper Johnny Horan was a passenger aboard an Air Force C-45 high above the Cascade Mountains in the state of Washington. He had hitched Air Force rides to the West Coast for a reunion in Seattle with his Japanese bride, Teruko, who was arriving in the United States with their three children the next day.

Five minutes later, the trip became a nightmare. The wings of the small aircraft started to ice, and the C-45 began to tilt to one side. Then the pilot ordered all aboard to bail out.

"I went first," said Horan. "I already had my parachute on. I weighed about 160 pounds. Add to that the weight of the chute and the heavy winter clothes I was wearing, and I estimate 200 pounds left that plane when I leaped out. It was my 29th jump."

The others on the plane were not forced to jump. After Horan bailed out, the plane righted itself. Without the 200 pounds Horan had added to the weight, the C-45 was able to land safely at a nearby Air Force base.

"I landed waist deep in snow. I folded up my chute, tucked it under my arm, and started downhill. I figured eventually I'd hit a highway. Little did I realize how long it would take me to get down off that mountain."

Darkness came and Horan kept moving. He didn't have any matches. All the brush he passed was damp or buried under the heavy snow anyway, so it was impossible for him to start a fire. His only course of action was to keep heading down the mountain. When daybreak arrived he was still completely surrounded by snow.

Finally—it was about eleven o'clock in the morning, which was the time his wife and children were due to arrive in Seattle aboard a ship—when, up ahead, he saw a small cabin. The snow was still waist deep and the little cabin seemed an eternity away. It took him more than an hour to reach the shelter.

The cabin was empty. The only food available was a can of cocoa. But there was a wood stove, an old bed, and a refrigerator, but no electricity.

Horan found some wood in a corner and started a fire in the stove with some matches he had found on a shelf. Then he melted some snow and enjoyed a cup of cocoa, after which he hung up his soaking wet clothes to dry.

In Seattle his wife and youngsters were aware by then that he was lost somewhere on the mountain.

"I did the only thing I could do," said Teruko. "I prayed for my husband's safe return."

Three days later her prayers were unanswered. A giant search had been conducted by the military and local authorities, but no trace of the paratrooper had been found.

Horan remained in the cabin for three days waiting for help to arrive. It never came.

"I was starving," he said. "The cocoa was gone, and I knew I'd have to do something if I wanted to survive. I decided to walk again."

"To do that, I figured I'd need snowshoes. So I tore off some large shingles from the cabin, and tied them to my boots with some cord from my chute. I was off again—but not for long. I got about a half-mile when the shingles broke on me. It was back to the cabin again. I started looking around for something else to try as snowshoes. I spotted the refrigerator shelf on the floor. There was

Example 2C (*Continued*)

a second shelf inside the icebox. I tied a shelf onto each of my boots. They seemed comfortable enough, so I was off again."

"This time my makeshift snowshoes worked. Those shelves kept me up on top of the snow, and I was able to move right along."

"Still, I had a long way to go. Night came, but I couldn't afford to stop. I was hungry; I was freezing too."

"The next day I was still moving. By then there was less snow. Only up to my knees, I'd guess. Still, there was nothing in sight except snow. I was beginning to get discouraged."

"Then I heard voices. Two men were talking and laughing. They were somewhere up ahead—beyond the trees. I shouted again and again. They heard me and came running through the snow toward me. They knew who I was the minute they saw me. There had been quite a bit in the newspapers about me."

"Those men picked me up, snowshoes and all, and carried me to a place called the Rustic Inn, which is on the outskirts of a small town called Easton. I remember the first thing I had was a cup of tea. It was the most delicious tea I ever tasted."

"I remember talking to my wife on the phone. Then an ambulance came, and they took me away to the hospital. I remember, just as they were carrying me out on the stretcher, asking one of the men to give me those two refrigerator shelves. 'They are the best Christmas present I ever had,' I told him. 'They saved my life.'"

Reprinted by permission from the 1984 edition of *The Old Farmer's Almanac*.

Main Idea List From "The Christmas I'll Never Forget"

1. On the way to meet his wife and family, John Horan's plane ices over and tilts to one side.

2. Horan parachutes out of the plane and enables it to safely land.

3. Horan finds a cabin, lives on cocoa until it is gone.

4. He decides to walk, tries to make snowshoes.

5. Shingles fail, but refrigerator shelves work, and he walks until he finds help.

6. The snowshoe shelves were the best Christmas present he ever had.

- **Main idea that is too general:** "Heart disease."
- **Main idea that is just right:** "Heart disease is on the decrease but is still No. 1."

Using the second sample news paragraph in Example 2A:

- **Main idea that is too specific:** "Homesteaders have to live there for 10 years."
- **Main idea that is too general:** "Free land."
- **Main idea that is just right:** "Free land offer nets big response."

The Goldilocks Technique adapts well as a classroom exercise. Teachers can record on the blackboard the different main ideas that students generate. Then through discussion and modeling, teachers can demonstrate which of the main ideas needs to be more specific, which needs to be more general, and which are just right. The class will discover that even for a "just right" main idea, there may be several different ways of stating it.

"Labeling the Bucket"

A second strategy that can be used to determine the main idea is called "labeling the bucket." With this technique, students are asked to draw or imagine a bucket. As they are categorizing, the individual words (items) will go into the bucket, and the students will come up with a label that best describes the contents of the bucket. As students are stating the main idea of a paragraph, the detail sentences will go into the bucket, and they will create a label that best describes the contents of the paragraph. When they are stating the section main idea of a multi-paragraph selection, the main ideas of all the paragraphs will go into the bucket, and students must come up with a label that best describes the content of the selection. Example 2D contains a visual that may be used to illustrate this strategy.

Self-Cueing

Self-cueing questions offer a third strategy for determining main ideas. First, students identify the general topic of a paragraph or multi-paragraph selection. Then they try to be more specific about what they are saying about this topic. Here is a series of questions a student can ask:

1. What is the one subject the author is talking about throughout the paragraph or selection? This is the topic.

Example 2D

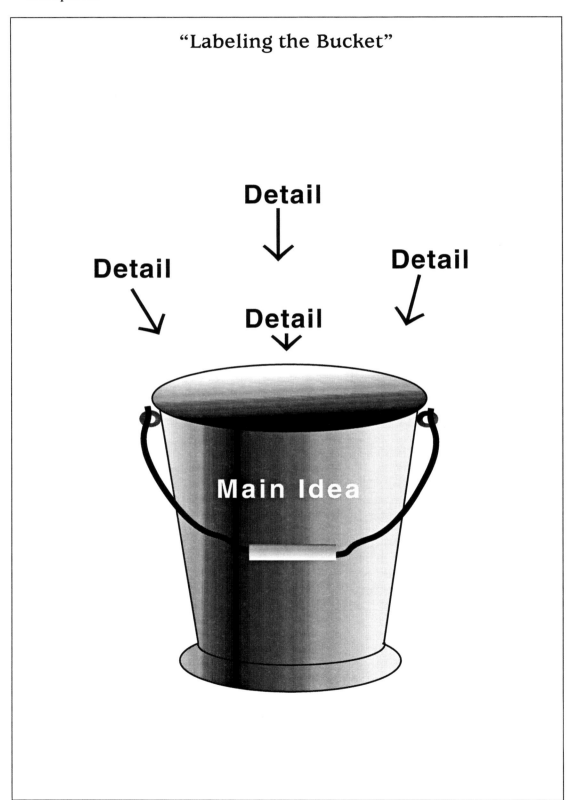

2. Are there any words or phrases that are repeated throughout the paragraph? If so, this may suggest the topic.

3. What is the author saying about this topic? This will help identify the main idea.

4. What do all the detail sentences have in common? This will help identify the main idea.

5. Is there a topic sentence that states this main idea? If so, copy or paraphrase it. (Remember: although the topic sentence is often the first sentence of the paragraph, it may also be found in the middle or at the end.)

6. If there is no topic sentence, create your own topic sentence.

7. Do all of the important details refer to the topic sentence you have chosen or created?

8. Check your main idea by asking if it is too general or too specific.

Main Ideas in Textbooks, Lengthy Selections, and Lesson Plans

At the beginning of this chapter, the organization of a supermarket was used as an example of how everyday things are organized by main ideas. The supermarket is also a good metaphor for the different roles that students and teachers play in applying main idea skills. The students are like the shopper; they must learn to figure out how the goods (details) in the store are organized in order to find what they need. They must also learn to use the help the store provides to identify those categories and to locate where they are found (the signs around the store and at the head of each aisle provide this guidance).

Conversely, teachers and authors' of textbooks are like the managers of a supermarket. If they do not adequately organize and present their product, then the students will have a harder time finding the goods (information they must learn). Just as supermarkets have departments with signs, teachers should group information into hierarchies of main ideas and label them by noting main ideas.

Let's use another analogy. The original Filene's Basement Store in Boston, Massachusetts is famous for being one of the original discount stores. All the products that did not sell in the main store were sent to the basement of the store where they were marked down progressively each week until they were sold. To accommodate the variety of inventory and to save costs, most merchandise was stacked on tables. Often there was no plan for display; a table of men's socks could be next to a table of women's skirts. While it was a great place to find a bargain, it was the worst place to shop if you needed something in particular because you could never find what you were looking for!

Sometimes the information in class lessons or in books is presented to students the way the old Filene's Basement would present its merchandise: lots of interesting details, but not much help in sorting things out. Educators have a responsibility, just like a good department store, to be sure their product is easy to find. As teachers plan lessons and choose material for subject matter, they should keep in mind main idea categories and the ease with which students will be able to identify them.

Textbooks and Lengthy Reading Selections

Many students, particularly those with a learning disability, get "lost in the details" when they are reading more than one page of information. Reviewing the main ideas before they read offers them an overall picture of what they will be reading. It gives them a "hook" on which to hang the details.

Most textbooks include unit and chapter titles, section headings, and several levels of sub-headings to help students organize information. Some publishers do an excellent job of stating main ideas, and they do so every three to eight paragraphs. Other publishers, however, produce text that is not as structured as it should be. Although paragraphs should contain one main idea, reading material sometimes includes one paragraph with several main ideas, or one main idea spread out over several paragraphs. Sometimes the section headings are either too specific or too general to help students.

It is important for teachers to preview textbooks and other material they will be using to determine how much structure is provided. If the textbook is structured well, teachers can simply create a preview sheet for students from a list of the headings to highlight the main ideas they will be encountering. If the material is not well structured, the teacher may have to develop a list of appropriate headings. To determine the level of structure provided, teachers should ask these questions:

- Are there good topic sentences, or do they have to be inferred?

- Are the paragraphs well structured, with one main idea per paragraph?

- Are the main ideas in a logical order?

- Has the book provided headings, sub-headings, and main idea questions?

Whenever a new chapter is introduced, the teacher should provide students with a pre-reading main idea list or chart. Sometimes textbooks provide an outline or graphic organizer that contains all the main ideas in a chapter. If this is the case, the teacher can simply copy it onto handouts or a slide for the overhead projector. If it is not provided, the teacher can develop her own chart. Example 2E is a main idea chart for this second chapter. Students should keep a copy of the chart in their notebooks and refer to it as they progress through the chapter. Teachers will find this chart is also helpful for parents or other educators who work with the students. The chart can eventually be used as a tool to organize information when studying for a chapter test.

Example 2E

Sample Main Idea Chart

Chapter 2, "Recognizing and Formulating Main Ideas"

1. Teaching main idea skills
   - Categorizing main ideas
   - Main ideas in paragraphs
   - Main ideas in multi-paragraph selections
2. Techniques for finding the main idea
   - Goldilocks
   - Labeling the bucket
   - Self-cueing
3. Main ideas in textbooks, lengthy selections, and lesson plans
   - Textbooks
   - Lengthy selections
   - Lesson Plans
4. Additional teaching strategies
   - Extract the most difficult paragraphs
   - Insert a sentence that does not belong
   - Scramble sentences
   - Find the main idea worksheet

Many classrooms no longer use textbooks. Instead, reading materials such as newspaper articles, text from websites, and student newsmagazines are used to supplement a thematic unit. If several sources are used, it may be more difficult for students to determine the main ideas than it is when reading from a textbook. In cases such as these, it is even more important to construct a main idea chart.

Main Ideas and Lesson Plans

Teachers often assume that students can see the "big picture" created by the pattern of daily lessons and believe that students will make connections between what was taught last week and this week. Many students, however, cannot make these connections. It is most helpful - especially for grades eight and above - for teachers to provide an overall outline of topics prior to a semester or unit of study. If students are following the Master Notebook System, these topic lists will be helpful when they cull through their working notebook to produce a cover sheet for the reserve accordion file (see Chapter 1). The outline of topics can also indicate which information students will learn from reading and which from class lectures. If it is possible, teachers should include a rough list of dates corresponding to the topic to be covered. These main idea planners are not only helpful to students, but many experienced teachers have also noted that these lists help organize their presentations!

Additional Teaching Suggestions

Extract and discuss the most difficult paragraphs as a pre-reading exercise

If there are certain paragraphs or passages that a teacher anticipates will be difficult for some students to understand, read these sections as a class and discuss the main ideas. Ask students to formulate the main ideas in their own words and the teacher can make a list of these responses on the board. Then elicit the important details from students and ask how these details support the main idea. Reviewing these paragraphs before students begin reading will get them started and improve their comprehension of the material.

Insert a sentence that does not belong

Teachers can take any structured paragraph that has a clear main idea and supporting details and add a sentence that does not belong. This forces students to look at each sentence to see if it supports the main idea in order to find the sentence that does not belong. This task also helps students learn to proofread their own compositions for good paragraph structure.

Scrambled Sentences

Teachers can scramble the sentences from a short selection containing several paragraphs with topic sentences. Students can reorder the sentences into paragraphs so that main ideas are supported by appropriate detail sentences. Then students can create a title (the topic) for the selection. In addition to practicing main idea skills, this type of exercise shows students how to arrange information when using notes to write a research paper.

Find the Main Idea Worksheet

This exercise guides students through the three steps for recognizing the main idea in a paragraph. Students can refer to this worksheet whenever they are identifying main ideas in paragraphs.

Main Idea Worksheet

Topic: (one or two words) _____

Main Idea: (what is the paragraph saying about the topic?) _____

_____

_____

Supporting Details: (list in phrase form)

_____
_____
_____
_____
_____
_____

CHAPTER 3

Note-Taking

Note-taking is a procedure for recording information from lectures or reading in order to retrieve that information later and study it. As students take notes, they become active learners because they must process information and explain it in their own words. Note-taking is also a valuable tool for gathering and organizing pieces of research for a report.

Taking notes, especially from lectures, is a difficult task for many students. Teachers often hear students say, "I can't keep up with the teacher," or "I can never understand my notes, so why study them?" Note-taking requires the integration of auditory processing skills (including auditory discrimination, processing rate, auditory short-term memory), visual-motor skills, writing skills (including spelling, handwriting, organization on the page), comprehension skills, and attention controls. With this range of skill requirements, it is easy to see why students become overwhelmed when they take notes, and in some cases, why they develop a fear of the task.

It is important to teach students the value of taking and studying notes on a consistent basis. Many students want to do the least schoolwork in the shortest amount of time. They believe that as long as they understand a lecture or information they have read, their memory will serve them well and taking notes is unnecessary. Until students see tangible success in the form of better test grades or higher quality papers, they may not be motivated to learn note-taking skills. Teachers should make taking notes mandatory and follow through by doing notebook checks in class. Teachers should help students develop the habit of automatically taking notes and copying information from the board by requiring them to take out their notebooks before class discussions. Assign note-taking along with readings for homework and provide time in class for starting these notes.

Teaching Note-Taking from Written Sources

Teachers should teach note-taking from written sources first until students have mastered the skill. Starting with written material eliminates auditory processing issues. Students can also go back over the information as often as needed, and they can take as much time as they need to process the information and write it into notes. Teachers can build student confidence about note-taking by using manageable written sources before moving on to notes from lectures.

Two-Column Method

When students have learned how to recognize and formulate main ideas, they can use this skill to take notes, including main ideas as well as details. A two-column format is the best method for noting and distinguishing main ideas from details. Two-column note-taking requires that a line be drawn down the length of each page of paper. One-third of the page is to the left of the line and two-thirds of the page is to the right. Main ideas are noted in the left column and details in the right. Example 3A provides an explanation of this method and can be given to students when two-column notes are introduced.

The two-column format provides a clear visual distinction between main ideas (on the left) and details (on the right). Outlines and graphic organizers also provide a visual distinction between main ideas and details—outlines by indenting five spaces, and graphic organizers by encircling each main idea. However, these formats are not as visually distinctive as the two-column format, especially for students who have visual perception difficulties. Most students find it hard to line up their outlines along imaginary margins, and the result is a steady stream of words that must be sorted out later. The drawback of using graphic organizers to take notes, especially from lectures, is that students must first know how many topics, sub-topics, and main ideas there will be in order to set up an appropriate visual web on the page. Also, if more than one page of notes is taken, the student loses the advantage of seeing how chunks of information are related on the page. Two-column note-taking has an advantage over both outlines and graphic organizers because it provides more space, especially in the main idea column, for adding information later. Although outlines and graphic organizers are excellent tools for organizing ideas before writing or for revising notes into study guides, two-column notes are more practical for initial note-taking.

Two-column notes are also handy for studying. The details on the right side of the page can be covered while the student reads each main idea and tries to remember the details. Likewise, the main ideas can be covered while the student uses the details to remember the main topics.

From Lists to Multi-Paragraph Selections

The progression for teaching main idea skills detailed in Chapter 2 (categorizing, single paragraphs with topic sentences, single paragraphs with inferred main ideas, multi-paragraph selections) should also be followed when introducing two-column note-taking. Teachers should begin with structured, short selections and progress to more complex, lengthy ma-

Example 3A

How to Take Two-Column Notes

Left 1/3 Page:	Right 2/3 Page:
Main Ideas	Details

1. List all details on the right side of the page.

   - Use as few words as possible

   - Use abbreviations

   - Use markers to connect details and underline important information

   - Skip lines as details change and leave extra space to add information later

2. Write main ideas and sub-main ideas on the left side of the page.

3. Go over your notes at the end of class or as soon as possible. Revise your notes and review the information.

4. Read through your notes in the evening and write study questions with answers.

terial. Some of the same materials used to teach main idea skills can be used to teach note-taking; the students will now be adding the details. For example, the categorizing lists from Chapter 2 would be noted as follows:

Main Ideas	Details
Fruit	apple
	orange
	banana
Emotions	anger
	love
	sadness
Colors	brown
	orange
	yellow
	blue
	green
Leaders of World War II Axis countries	Hitler (Germany)
	Mussolini (Italy)
	Tojo (Japan)
Leaders of World War II Allied countries	Churchill (England)
	Roosevelt (United States)
	Stalin (U.S.S.R.)

At the paragraph level, teachers can demonstrate how the stated or implied main idea should be written on the left side of the notes and the supporting sentences on the right side (see Example 3B for an illustration of this skill at the paragraph level).

Once students are familiar with note-taking at the paragraph level, they can practice taking notes from multi-paragraph material. If teachers use structured material with one main idea per paragraph, students' notes

Example 3B

Behavior of Groups

There are many reasons why people affiliate, or join, with others in groups. We are members of a family group by birth or adoption. We join clubs because we like to sing, ski, hike, or participate in some other activity a group offers. If you go to a crowded football game, you have a kind of fun you could not have by yourself. People tend to join groups when danger threatens, because in associating with others they feel more secure. Also, it is only by joining with others and working together that people can achieve certain goals, such as persuading their senator to support a certain bill or raising money for their senior class.

Raglan and Saxon, *Invitation to Psychology*, 1985. This material is reproduced by permission of Scott, Foresman and Company.

Main Idea	Details
○ Reasons why people group together	• Born or adopted into a family group • To participate in group activity • Can have more fun in groups • Can feel more secure in a group • To get help in achieving goals
○	
○	

will reflect the same number of main ideas in the left column of their notes. Example 3C illustrates how the details from the article "Juvenile Juries" in Chapter 2 can be added to the main ideas to form notes.

Example 3C

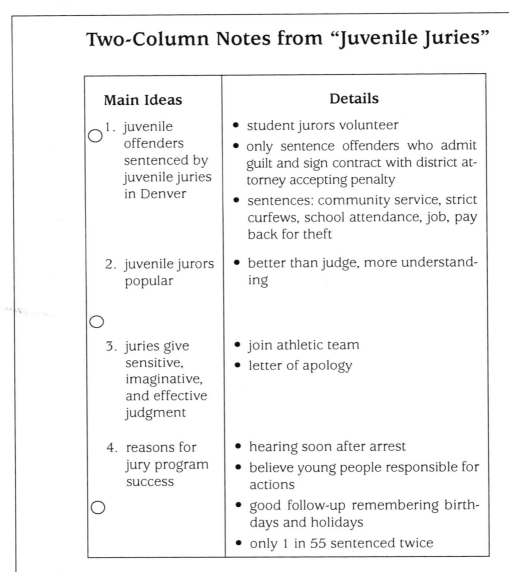

Two-Column Notes from "Juvenile Juries"

Main Ideas	Details
1. juvenile offenders sentenced by juvenile juries in Denver	• student jurors volunteer • only sentence offenders who admit guilt and sign contract with district attorney accepting penalty • sentences: community service, strict curfews, school attendance, job, pay back for theft
2. juvenile jurors popular	• better than judge, more understanding
3. juries give sensitive, imaginative, and effective judgment	• join athletic team • letter of apology
4. reasons for jury program success	• hearing soon after arrest • believe young people responsible for actions • good follow-up remembering birthdays and holidays • only 1 in 55 sentenced twice

Once students have learned to apply two-column note-taking skills using structured material, they should practice taking notes from less structured reading selections. Teachers should provide selections from textbook chapters, magazine articles, newspaper stories, encyclopedias, and web-site material for practice. Example 3D is a sample of two-column notes taken from the text of President Bill Clinton's inaugural address. Because it is the text from a speech, it is more challenging to determine the main ideas and details than it is from textbook material that is designed specifically for student study.

Example 3D

President Bill Clinton's First Inaugural Address

My fellow citizens, today we celebrate the mystery of American renewal. This ceremony is held in the depth of winter, but by the words we speak and the faces we show the world, we force the spring. A spring reborn in the world's oldest democracy, that brings forth the vision and courage to reinvent America. When our founders boldly declared America's independence to the world, and our purposes to the Almighty, they knew that America, to endure, would have to change. Not change for change sake, but change to preserve America's ideals: life, liberty, the pursuit of happiness.

Though we march to the music of our time, our mission is timeless. Each generation of Americans must define what it means to be an American. On behalf of our nation, I salute my predecessor, President Bush, for his half-century of service to America . . . and I thank the millions of men and women whose steadfastness and sacrifice triumphed over depression, fascism and communism.

Today, a generation raised in the shadows of the Cold War assumes new responsibilities in a world warmed by the sunshine of freedom, but threatened still by ancient hatreds and new plagues. Raised in unrivaled prosperity, we inherit an economy that is still the world's strongest, but is weakened by business failures, stagnant wages, increasing inequality, and deep divisions among our own people.

When George Washington first took the oath I have just sworn to uphold, news traveled slowly across the land by horseback, and across the ocean by boat. Now the sights and sounds of this ceremony are broadcast instantaneously to billions around the world. Communications and commerce are global. Investment is mobile.

Technology is almost magical, and ambition for a better life is now universal.

We earn our livelihood in America today in peaceful competition with people all across the Earth. Profound and powerful forces are shaking and remaking our world, an urgent question of our time is whether we can make change our friend and not our enemy. This new world has already enriched the lives of millions of Americans who are able to compete and win in it. But when most people are working harder for less, when others cannot work at all, when the cost of health care devastates and threatens to bankrupt our enterprises, great and small; when the fear of crime robs law abiding citizens of their freedom; and when millions of poor children cannot even imagine the lives we are calling them to lead, we have not made change our friend.

We know we have to face hard truths and take strong steps, but we have not done so. Instead we have drifted, and that drifting has eroded our resources, fractured our economy, and shaken our confidence. Though our challenges are fearsome, so are our strengths. Americans have ever been a restless, questing, hopeful people, and we must bring to our task today the vision and will of those who came before us. From our Revolution to the Civil War, to the Great Depression, to the Civil Rights movement, our people have always mastered the determination to construct from these crises the pillars of our history. Thomas Jefferson believed that to preserve the very foundations of our nation we would need dramatic changes from time to time. Well, my fellow Americans, this is our time. Let us embrace it.

Our democracy must be not only the envy of the world but the engine of our own renewal.

Example 3D (*Continued*)

There is nothing wrong with America that cannot be cured by what is right with America.

And so today we pledge an end to the era of deadlock and drift, and a new season of American renewal has begun.

To renew America we must be bold. We must do what no generation has had to do before. We must invest more in our own people, in their jobs, and in their future, and at the same time cut our massive debt . . . and we must do so in a world in which we must compete for every opportunity. It will not be easy. It will require sacrifice, but it can be done, and done fairly. Not choosing sacrifice for its own sake, but for our own sake. We must provide for our nation the way a family provides for its children. Our founders saw themselves in the light of posterity. We can do no less. Anyone who has ever watched a child's eyes wander into sleep knows what posterity is. Posterity is the world to come, the world for whom we hold our ideals, from whom we have borrowed our planet, and to whom we bear sacred responsibilities. We must do what America does best, offer more opportunity to all and demand more responsibility from all.

It is time to break the bad habit of expecting something for nothing: from our government, or from each other. Let us all take more responsibility, not only for ourselves and our families, but for our communities and our country. To renew America we must revitalize our democracy. This beautiful capitol, like every capitol since the dawn of civilization, is often a place of intrigue and calculation. Powerful people maneuver for position and worry endlessly about who is in and who is out, who is up and who is down, forgetting those people whose toil and sweat sends us here and paves our way.

Americans deserve better, and in this city today there are people who want to do better, and so I say to all of you here, let us resolve to reform our politics, so that power and privilege no longer shout down the voice of the people. Let us put aside personal advantage, so that we can feel the pain and see the promise of America. Let us resolve to make our government a place for what Franklin Roosevelt called "bold, persistent experimentation, a government for our tomorrow's, not our yesterdays." Let us give this capitol back to the people to whom it belongs.

To renew America we must meet challenges abroad, as well as at home. There is no longer a clear division between what is foreign and what is domestic. The world economy, the world environment, the world AIDS crisis, the world arms race: they affect us all. Today as an old order passes, the new world is more free, but less stable. Communism's collapse has called forth old animosities, and new dangers. Clearly, America must continue to lead the world we did so much to make. While America rebuilds at home, we will not shrink from the challenges nor fail to seize the opportunities of this new world. Together with our friends and allies, we will work together to shape change, lest it engulf us. When our vital interests are challenged, or the will and conscience of the international community is defied, we will act; with peaceful diplomacy whenever possible, with force when necessary. The brave Americans serving our nation today in the Persian Gulf, in Somalia, and wherever else they stand, are testament to our resolve, but our greatest strength is the power of our ideas, which are still new in many lands. Across the world, we see them embraced and we rejoice. Our hopes, our hearts, our hands, are with those on every continent, who are building democracy and freedom. Their cause is America's cause. The American people have summoned the change we celebrate today. You have raised your voices in an unmistakable chorus, you have cast your votes in historic numbers, you have changed the face of congress, the presidency, and the political process itself. Yes, you, my fellow Americans, have forced the spring. Now we must do the work the season demands. To that work I now turn with all the authority of my office. I ask congress to join with me; but no president, no congress, no government can undertake this mission alone.

My fellow Americans, you, too, must play your part in our renewal. I challenge a new generation of young Americans to a season of service, to act on your idealism, by helping troubled children, keeping company with those in need, reconnecting our torn communities. There is so much to be done. Enough, indeed, for millions of others who are still young in spirit, to give of

Example 3D (*Continued*)

themselves in service, too. In serving we recognize a simple, but powerful, truth: we need each other, and we must care for one another. Today we do more than celebrate America, we rededicate ourselves to the very idea of America, an idea born in revolution, the knowledge that but for fate, we, the fortunate and the unfortunate, might have been each other; an idea ennobled by the faith that our nation can summon from its myriad diversity, the deepest measure of unity; an idea infused with the conviction that America's long, heroic journey must go forever upward.

And so, my fellow Americans, as we stand at the edge of the 21st Century, let us begin anew, with energy and hope, with faith and discipline, and let us work until our work is done. The Scripture says: "And let us not be weary in well-doing, for in due season we shall reap, if we faint not." From this joyful mountaintop of celebration we hear a call to service in the valley. We have heard the trumpets, we have changed the guard, and now each in our own way, and with God's help, we must answer the call. Thank you, and God bless you all.

NOTES

Main Ideas	Details
○ We celebrate the mystery of American renewal— America has to change	
Americans must assume new responsibilities in a world of problems	• ancient hatreds and new plagues • economy weakened by business failure, stagnant wages • increasing inequality and deep divisions among our own people
○ Powerful forces are remaking our world	• communications and commerce are global • investment is mobile • technology is almost magical
Make change our friend, not our enemy	
There are other problems	• people working harder for less • others cannot work at all • cost of health care • fear of crime • millions of poor children
○ Have to face truths and take strong steps	• challenges are fearsome, but so are our strengths

Example 3D (*Continued*)

Main Ideas	Details
To renew America, we must	• be bold • invest more in our own people • cut massive debt • take more responsibility • revitalize our democracy • reform our politics • put aside personal advantage
We must also face challenges abroad	• world economy • world environment • AIDS crisis • world arms race

We must continue to lead the world	• shape change
	• get involved when
	  1. vital interests are challenged
	  2. if the conscience of the international community is defied
	• use peaceful diplomacy when possible, force when necessary

Challenge of service to young Americans	• so much to be done • we need each other, must care for one another
As we begin the 21st Century	• let's begin anew • with energy and hope, faith and discipline • until work is done

Some students when taking notes write everything down and have trouble identifying irrelevant information. Others may have difficulty including enough important information in their notes. An open note quiz is one way that students can test their notes to see if they are complete. Students must use their notes to find answers; credit is given for a correct answer only when it can be found in the notes. This exercise underscores the importance of taking thorough notes. After the quiz, teachers should ask students which questions dealt more with a main idea (from notes on the left side) or which dealt with facts, examples, and definitions (from notes on the right side). This will help illustrate the usefulness of studying both the main ideas and details in notes.

Models of two-column notes should be available so students can see what their notes should look like. Teachers should distribute a copy of notes with reading selections and then explain how information was pulled from the paragraphs and developed into notes. Assign a similar selection for homework. The next day, hand out a sample of teacher-generated notes so students can compare and analyze their work. Pair students up and encourage them to exchange notes to determine if important information was left out or if irrelevant information should be removed. Teachers can also hand out a partially completed note sheet and instruct students to fill in the missing main ideas and details.

Teachers should encourage class discussion about notes. Plan a lesson where the students observe the teacher taking notes on the board based on student suggestions. Once students get used to working as a group, they will not hesitate to disagree with one another. Also, working as a class provides a good opportunity to show students how notes can be fine-tuned.

Note-Taking Sub-Skills

There are three sub-skills that students must learn to be good note-takers:

1. Abbreviating

2. Paraphrasing information into short phrases

3. Using visual markings to organize notes

Teachers frequently assume that students have learned these basic skills, especially by the time they reach high school. However, many students need specific instruction in these areas. It is hard to believe that a sixteen-year-old would not know that "Mr." is an abbreviation for "Mister," or "vs." for "versus," but if you ask students to abbreviate a list of common words, you may be surprised to see how many lack this skill.

Commonly accepted abbreviations such as the two previous examples, as well as symbols ("w/" for "with" and " + " for "and") should be reviewed. Teachers should encourage students to use the first syllable or part of a word instead of writing out full words ("cap" for "capital" or "subj" for "subject"). Omitting vowels from some words is also a good way to abbreviate ("prps" for "purpose"). Teachers should pass out a list of common abbreviations and require that students refer to the list during note-taking lessons. When modeling notes on the board, suggest abbreviations for terms that come up regularly in the material. For homework, give students lists of words to abbreviate or lists of abbreviations that they must turn back into words. Divide the class into teams and have contests with abbreviation exercises. Learning how to use abbreviations automatically will save time and writing energy, especially when taking notes from lectures.

Paraphrasing information into short phrases is also a necessary note-taking skill. Just as fourth and fifth grade students are finally learning the rule "you must write in complete sentences," they are beginning to be required to take notes when complete sentences are impractical. Students tend to copy whole sentences from their reading or try to write every word from a lecture. One way to practice writing notes using a minimum of words is to "telegraph" sentences. Give students a set of notes with the main ideas and details stated in full sentences. Ask them to eliminate unnecessary words and make abbreviations. A class game can be played where students are charged points for every letter and word they use to translate a sentence into a telegraph note. Students compete to see who has the fewest points from notes that are still readily understood by class members. When reviewing student notes, teachers should draw lines through words and phrases that are not necessary. Students can also exchange notes and check each other's work for economy of words.

Finally, teachers should show students how to use visual markings to improve the visual organization of notes on the page. Some suggestions:

- Draw lines horizontally across the page to emphasize the change from one main idea to the next

- Use colored markers to highlight important information

- Number the order of details

- Leave space after each main idea so information can be added later

- Add arrows, stars, and brackets to show connections between ideas in the notes

Teaching Note-Taking from Lectures and Non-Written Sources

When taking notes from a written source, students can go back over the material to be sure they have all the important information, and they can read and write notes at their own pace. However, taking notes from a lecture, class discussion, movie, or other non-written source is more difficult because the student cannot control the rate at which the material is presented or take time to preview the material.

Teachers sometimes think that skills for taking notes from lectures are not needed until high school because elementary teachers do not give formal lectures. However, when instruction in good listening and note-taking skills begins in the early grades, students gradually develop the ability to take notes from more advanced oral presentations in later grades.

Given the difficulty of the task and the fact that some students have developed an aversion to taking notes, it is particularly important that teachers use structured assignments that are geared for success. Teach the skill one step at a time and provide a lot of practice until students feel confident about their ability to take notes from oral sources.

During an oral lesson, teachers should use the blackboard to model the process by writing the main ideas on the left side and details on the right. A list of the main ideas may also be put on the board before the presentation begins. This will help students anticipate the details. Teachers can hand out a two-column page of notes and ask students to follow along. As students develop note-taking skills, provide partially completed notes from a lecture, which students must complete during the lecture. Eventually, teachers should provide only a skeleton page with blank spaces where the student must add the main ideas and details.

Introduce lecture note-taking by conducting a short, preplanned oral presentation that has one clear main idea and a few details. Present the information orally three times. The first time, students should listen without taking notes. The second time, they should identify the main idea and write it down, and the third time, they should listen for the details and write them down. Depending on student abilities, the teacher might need to micro-unit this task even further by telling the students how many details there will be.

Next, give an oral presentation that closely follows a structured, multi-paragraph selection with several main ideas. Repeat the presentation several times so students can take notes on main ideas and then details. Provide enough practice with this type of material so students feel confident about note-taking at this level. As presentations become more complex, teachers can show students how to leave spaces in their notes and use question marks if they feel they have missed something; they should be encouraged to ask the teacher or a fellow classmate for this information after the lecture. Teach students to continue writing details in the right column even if they are not sure what the main idea is. Main ideas are sometimes formulated and added in the left column later, especially if the speaker does not state the main point at the beginning of the presentation.

Once students become adept at listening for main ideas and details, teachers can present more difficult and varied material for note-taking practice. A presentation can be recorded on a tape machine and segments of the talk reviewed by using the pause and reverse controls of the recorder. This type of exercise provides time for class discussion about how notes should be taken. Use a videotaped recording of a newscast or other informational program that can be stopped and played back to discuss the application of note-taking skills. When lecturing, teachers can stop to ask, "What was the main idea of what I said?" or, "How many details did I just give to support my point?" When teachers take the time to talk about how notes are taken and follow through by checking student notes on a regular basis, it is time well spent. Students will respond by developing the ability to take notes independently.

Notes from an Interview

Another way to introduce notes from oral sources is to give students the opportunity to take notes from an interview. The interview provides the advantage of student control; the student can determine the main ideas (questions) ahead of time. They can also exercise some control over the pace of the oral responses by finishing their notes to one question before asking the next. Students can interview each other, parents, friends, or teachers. Example 3E provides questions to interview a family member. The questions should be written in the left column as main ideas, and the answers become the details in the right column.

Students can also be assigned to take notes from a scene. They choose a place where they can take notes on what is happening (such as lunch in the cafeteria or study hall in the library). Main idea questions (Who is in the room? What are they doing?) are written ahead of time in the left column, and the detail notes are taken in the right.

Recognizing Speaker Cues

Speakers often provide verbal or body language cues that can help note-takers identify important information. Teach students to be aware of the following cues:

1. A speaker usually pauses before moving on to a new main idea.

2. When something is repeated or emphasized, it is usually important and should be included in the notes.

3. Transitional words such as "next," "finally," and "the most important," signal important information or an organizational pattern that a speaker may be using (listing information, comparing and contrasting information, or describing).

Example 3E

Note-Taking from an Interview

Main Ideas = Questions	Details = Answers
○ What are the names and ages of the people in your family?	
Can you describe a job or hobby for each member of your family?	
○ Where does your family live? Have they ever lived somewhere else?	
Can you tell me three interesting things about your family? ○	

4. A speaker provides organizational cues through body language (shifting weight, looking back at notes, pointing, looking more directly at the audience).

5. Changes in volume, pace, or inflection of the speaker's voice may indicate a change in the main idea or emphasize important details.

6. Introductory and concluding remarks often provide a good summary of the main ideas in the presentation.

Teachers should take a moment during lectures and class discussions to point out examples of these types of cues. Many students are not aware of these simple but helpful tips.

Example 3F lists steps to follow when taking notes from a lecture. It can be given to students and reviewed whenever they are about to take notes from a lecture.

"Note-Taking" versus "Note-Making"

The first step in effective note-taking is to get the important information down in an organized format (note-taking). This chapter provides suggestions for using the two-column method for note-taking. However, students must actively revise and review notes in order to commit the information to long-term memory (note-making). Chapter 6, "Study and Mastery: The Master Notebook System," contains suggestions for how to edit notes, create study questions, develop summaries, and apply other note-making strategies to learn and master the information.

If notes are edited and reviewed within 24 hours of being recorded, there will be significantly more carry-over to long-term memory than if students wait. Notes should also be reviewed soon after they are taken so students can determine if they need to ask a fellow student or the teacher for information they may have missed. When students realize they have fallen behind and missed information, they should mark that spot in the notes with a question mark and then skip several lines before continuing to take notes. This will provide space to add information later.

When taking notes from lectures, it is also helpful to write only on the front side of the page. As students come to the bottom of the page, they should turn the page, leave its backside blank, and begin taking notes on the next page. This will leave a blank work page for each page of notes; this space can be used during note-making to write questions or summaries (see Chapter 6).

Example 3F

How to Listen and Take Notes from a Lecture

1. Anticipate what the lecturer will discuss

   — review notes from the previous lecture

   — complete related readings before you come to class

   — refer to any handouts the teacher gives before or during the lecture

2. Use the two-column format and take organized notes

   — listen for main ideas by asking, "What is the point of this?"

   — listen for details by asking "Is this information relevant, and does it support the main idea?"

   — abbreviate and use simple phrasing

   — use lines and other visual markers to separate, emphasize and organize notes

3. Look for cues from the speaker

   — notice body language (shifts in position, pauses, etc,)

   — listen for signal and transitional words such as "the next..." "first...second...final" "there are four reasons..."

   — be sure to note remarks that are repeated or emphasized

4. Be an active listener

   — sit close to the speaker so you can see and hear better

   — leave room in your notes for information you missed and ask clarifying questions during or after the lecture

Selective Note-Taking

When students take notes from sources for a research report or special project, they will need to apply selective note-taking skills. When taking notes from lectures or reading assignments, students usually need to note all important information. However, when collecting research notes, students must sort through a large body of information and select only information that pertains to their topic.

Selective note-taking skills are used at elementary through college levels. A fourth grade student who is preparing a one-page report about beagles applies selective note-taking as he reads an encyclopedia entry about dogs. A high school senior uses selective note-taking to gather evidence from several news articles to support a debate position. Teachers should not take for granted that students will develop successful selective note-taking strategies on their own; these skills can and should be taught.

Teachers should introduce selective note-taking by choosing a structured reading selection about a topic with two opposing viewpoints, such as the pros and cons of children watching television. Students should read the selection and highlight information that supports one side of the issue (i.e., watching television is helpful). Students can then copy this information into two-column notes. Next, they should use a different color highlighter to identify information which supports the opposing view (i.e., watching television is harmful). Later, students can use their notes from this exercise to stage a class debate.

Teachers can develop a selective note-taking exercise for students using an encyclopedia entry about a major city. First, choose a subtopic, such as the history of the city, and instruct students to search for information that pertains just to this subtopic. There may be a specific section in the entry just for history; this is where students will find most of the information on this subtopic. However, information may also be found about the history of the city in other, less obvious sections of the entry. Encourage students to read the entire encyclopedia entry carefully to search and highlight relevant information. Try doing a city together as a class assignment by reading sections together and asking the class if material should be noted or not. Then assign another city for students to research by themselves. Eventually, students can use their notes to write a short report about the history of one of these cities.

Once students can take notes on a specific topic from one source, the teacher should require students to take notes on a topic from several sources. For example, a sixth grade teacher can give students material about lobsters from the following sources:

- A dictionary entry

- A short encyclopedia entry

- A paragraph from a cookbook on lobsters

- A section from an article about lobstermen

Choose a subtopic, such as the physical description of lobsters or the many ways to use lobsters. Students should read the sources and highlight only the information that pertains to that subtopic. Highlighted information should be reduced to note phrases and organized into main ideas and supporting details on a note page or note card. Some sources will contain a lot of information that should go in the notes, while others may contain very little.

This assignment can be made more challenging for older students by using longer, more complex resources. For example, teachers can choose a famous American and collect information for the class about that person from an encyclopedia, a book of facts and dates, an annotated biography, a general American history book, and another source such as a political or art history book. Assign several subtopics about this person to individuals or teams of students. Students should selectively take notes on subtopics such as childhood, family life, specific accomplishments, or monuments dedicated to the person's achievements. Teachers should take the students through the process step-by-step and encourage them to explain why they have included each piece of data. Later, the notes can be used to write a report about the famous individual.

Skeleton Notes of Main Ideas/Graphic Organizers

Although the two-column method is an excellent approach for introducing note-taking and works well with short reading selections and lecures, students need a different approach for noting layers of main ideas in lengthier material such as a textbook. Taking two-column notes paragraph-by-paragraph from a twenty-page chapter is cumbersome and time consuming. By forming a skeleton outline of main ideas, students can quickly create an overview of the main points and note how they relate to each other. To create a skeleton outline, students apply advanced main idea skills to determine the hierarchy of main ideas. As they read, they should ask the following questions:

- What is the main topic of the chapter?

- How many sections (main categories of information) are in the chapter?

- How many main ideas make up each section?

- What specific main ideas are presented in the paragraphs?

Most textbooks use larger, bold print to indicate titles of chapters, major sections, and main points within these sections. Teachers should instruct students to use these headings to help determine the main ideas. They should create an outline or a graphic organizer with these main ideas that will show at a glance how the material in the chapter is organized. Example 3G is a skeleton list of the main ideas in this chapter turned into a graphic organizer. A similar outline of main ideas can be created from a week's worth of lecture notes, or from combinations of main ideas from several sources used in class. These overview notes of main concepts provide a structured, micro-united approach for reviewing information and studying for a test.

Additional Teaching Strategies

Suggestion 1: Prepare Pre-lecture Questions
Hand out questions before giving a lecture or assigning a reading. Divide the questions into those that can be answered with main ideas and those that can be answered with details. Using the two-column format, place the main idea questions in the left column and detail questions in the right. Students should listen or read for the answers and then write the answers to the questions on a separate two-column note page. This assignment will reinforce listening and reading with a purpose, as well as help students group information for notes into main ideas and details.

Suggestion 2: Assign Oral Presentations
Require students to prepare and give brief oral presentations to the class. The topics can be something of personal interest, such as "show and tell" talks, or a more formal presentation of material from the textbook or other reference sources. Teachers should encourage presenters to organize their material into clear main ideas and details so other students can take notes. While the student presents, take two-column notes on the board as a model. In addition to providing an opportunity to model note-taking skills, this technique helps students become used to different presentation styles and rates of speaking.

Similarly, students can use the notes they take from the lecture to retell that lecture the next day or later in the week.

Example 3G

Graphic Organizer for Chapter 3

Note-Taking

1. Introduction

1. note-taking records information and is a tool for gathering research
2. a difficult task
3. need to teach and practice on consistent basis

2. Teaching Note-Taking from Written Sources

Two-Column Method

1. line down page—1/3 on left for main ideas, 2/3 on right for details
2. outlining and graphic organizers
3. advantages of two-column
4. handy for study

From Lists to Multi-Paragraph Selections

1. categorizing
2. paragraph level—stated and implied topic sentences
3. multi-paragraphs
4. use less structured material
5. open notes quiz to test notes
6. provide models of notes
7. encourage class discussion about notes

3. Note-Taking Sub-Skills

1. abbreviating
2. paraphrasing into short phrases
3. using visual markers

4. Teaching Note-Taking from Lectures and Non-Written Sources

1. more difficult than written sources
2. model on the board
3. introduce using short, structured lectures
4. move to longer lectures
5. Notes from an Interview
   - advantage is that students can control
   - notes from a scene
6. Recognizing Speaker Cues
   - verbal and body language

5. Note-Taking vs. Note-Making

1. note-taking is getting information down in an organized way
2. note-making is active revision to move to long-term memory
3. edit and review within 24 hours
4. write notes on one side of page—other side used for study

6. Selective Note-Taking

1. research requires selective note-taking
2. useful from 4th grade up
3. start with pro/con information from one selection
4. move to encyclopedia selection with several sub-topics
5. move to multiple sources

7. Skeleton Notes of Main Ideas, Graphic Organizers

1. use skeleton notes of main ideas for lengthy materials, textbooks
2. use textbook headings to create graphic organizer

8. Additional Teaching Strategies

1. pre-lecture questions
2. assign oral presentations
3. review main ideas
4. prioritize notes for study

Suggestion 3: Review Main Ideas

Write main ideas on the blackboard before or during a lecture. Keep the notes there until the next day. Begin the next day's lesson by pointing to each main idea and asking students to provide details based on their notes from the day before. At this time, students should add to their notes any information covered in this review that they initially missed. Encourage them to use their notes to provide answers instead of simply relying on memory.

Suggestion 4: Prioritize Notes for Study

When studying for a test, some students do not know how much emphasis to place on various topics presented during a chapter. As a result, they may over-study small details and insufficiently review major blocks of information. Good notes should reflect the emphasis a teacher places on material. During review sessions, teachers should show students how to apportion their study time for different topics based on the emphasis given in class. This extra time and attention to a topic should be reflected in their notes. When handing back a quiz or test, show students where the information on the test can be found in their notes.

CHAPTER 4

Summarizing and Paraphrasing

Summarizing and paraphrasing are skills that require students to reprocess information and express it in their own words. These skills enhance student comprehension because they require active reading and listening. They also lead to long-term mastery of information as students go beyond simply understanding to being able to express that understanding.

A summary is an overview, in the student's words, of the most important information from reading, lectures, or multi-media sources. Sometimes there is so much information that students get lost in the details; a summary enables them to see the greater picture. A summary is always shorter than the original material. A paraphrase is also written in the student's own words, but it is a restatement of the original information and is therefore as long (or longer) than the original material. A summary is based primarily on main ideas, while a paraphrase includes details.

Teaching Summarizing Skills

Teachers should introduce summarizing by discussing how it is a useful skill outside the classroom. Today's society places a premium on being able to get to the point, and there are many examples in daily work, family, and social life that call for summarizing. Business people want to know the "bottom line," doctors must summarize a condition and course of treatment, attorneys can win cases with good summaries, and newscasters summarize the day's events. We appreciate the friend who gives us a good summary of the movie we are thinking of seeing, but we might not ask his opinion again if all he gives us is a lot of details that are out of sequence.

Just about anything in school can be summarized: a class lecture, an essay, a news article, a movie or filmstrip, an historic event, a scientific process, a short story, or even a varsity basketball game. Keep in mind that the task of summarizing is not easy for students to learn. They need micro-united steps to follow, continuous practice with each step, and consistent feedback and monitoring.

Using Two-Column Notes
In order to write a summary, a student must first identify the main ideas. Begin teaching summarizing skills by using two-column notes as a basis for

creating a simple summary. The main ideas from the left side of the note-taking page form a basic outline; the student turns these main idea phrases into sentences to write a summary. The summary in Example 4A was developed using the notes from "Juvenile Juries" (complete article on page 29). In this instance, the main ideas from the left column and a few supporting details from the right column are turned into sentences to create a concise summary of the original article.

Example 4A

Summary of "Juvenile Juries" (from Example 2B)

Juvenile offenders in Denver are being sentenced by juvenile jurors. The juvenile jurors are popular because offenders feel they receive a fairer sentence than they would receive from a judge. These juries have given sensitive, imagi-native, and effective judgments. The program is considered successful because kids receive a hearing soon after the arrest, and the district attorney's office provides good follow-up.

While "Juvenile Juries" easily lends itself to summarizing due to its brevity and one main idea per paragraph, some summaries are more challenging, such as President Clinton's inaugural address, which is summarized in Example 4B (complete address on page 47).

Example 4B

Summary of Bill Clinton's First Inaugural Address (from Example 3D)

Americans must assume new responsibilities in a world with problems, including old hatreds, weak economies, and increasing inequality. There are powerful forces remaking our world, including global communications, commerce, and new technology. We should try to use these changes positively.

There are problems we must face in our country, such as not enough work, cost of health care, crime, and children in poverty. To face these problems we must be strong, invest in our people, cut debt, take more responsibility, and reform politics.

Americans must also meet challenges abroad, including problems in the world economy, the environment, the AIDS crisis, and the arms race. To shape world change, Americans must get involved using peaceful diplomacy when possible, and with force when necessary.

President Clinton challenges young Americans to become involved and care for one another. He urges Americans to have energy and hope as we begin the 21st Century.

There are a variety of ways to encourage students to practice writing summaries. Students can use two-column notes from previous lessons to practice writing summaries, or as they take notes, teachers can ask them to use these notes to write a summary. With high school students, teachers can require that students write summaries from lecture notes as a way to develop good habits for study and note review.

Some students may have difficulty organizing the main ideas into logical categories and writing them into a unified paragraph. While it takes practice, it is helpful if students realize a few things about summarizing. First, students must learn that the order of main ideas is flexible once they are taken out of the text. Also, two main ideas may be combined into one sentence, or the last main idea may become the topic sentence of the summary. There is no set formula for determining the order of main ideas, so the best way to teach summarizing is through modeling and class discussion. Example 4C lists the six steps to write a summary.

Example 4C

How to Write a Summary

1. Read the material and distinguish the main ideas from the details.

2. List the main ideas in phrase form.

3. Group the main ideas into logical categories — the order in which you read the main ideas is not always the best order for writing a summary.

4. Turn the main ideas into sentences and combine them into a paragraph using transitional words. Include a topic sentence.

5. Proofread a first draft for punctuation, spelling, and unity.

6. Make a final copy with neat handwriting.

Summarizing requires the application of good, basic writing techniques. Students may need reminders to begin paragraphs with topic sentences and to write in complete sentences. Transitional words are useful for connecting ideas in a summary. See Example 1E on page 13 for some common transitional words.

Using a Variety of Materials

As students develop their summarizing skills, teachers should use less-structured material that is longer and more complex for summary practice. Summaries from scientific material may be harder to write than summaries from social studies material, or vice versa, so teachers should be sure to give students practice summarizing material from different subject areas. Here are some suggestions for integrating summarizing skills into classroom work:

1. When reviewing material in class, ask questions that require students to summarize information.

2. Give students prepared summaries as models of what was covered in class during the week.

3. At the end of a lecture, or as a review of an assigned reading, require the class to create a summary through group discussion and write it on the board.

4. Ask students to present oral summaries as reviews of assigned readings or previous lectures.

Literature, such as short stories, biographies, or novels, provides another opportunity for writing summaries. These sources allow students to write plot summaries based on a list of main events. Example 4D is a plot summary of the story "The Christmas I'll Never Forget" (complete story found on page 31).

Example 4D

Summary of "The Christmas I'll Never Forget" (from Example 2C)

John M. Horan keeps a pair of refrigerator shelves and puts them under his tree every Christmas because they saved his life. Years ago, when he was flying over Washington State on the way to meet his family at Christmas time, the plane he was in experienced trouble, and he parachuted out. He fell safely to earth and walked in search of a highway. He came to a cabin and waited there for help until the cocoa, his only source of food, ran out. He needed snowshoes to walk for help, so he made them out of shelves from the refrigerator. With the help of the shelves, he was able to walk until hunters rescued him. John Horan considers those shelves — which saved his life — his best Christmas present ever.

Reading or listening to student summaries is one way of knowing which students really understand the content and which need more instruction. Writing summaries on a daily and weekly basis will ensure consistent and steady review of information, and the summaries can be used later as overviews when studying for a test.

Teaching Paraphrasing Skills

Paraphrasing is the process of restating information in different words. When we paraphrase, we maintain the original meaning, but we say it in our own words. Paraphrasing is an active learning strategy which helps us place information into long-term memory as we move from an understanding level to an active comprehension level. Good paraphrasing skills are necessary to create effective summaries, prepare for tests, answer essay test questions, and avoid plagiarism when researching reports. Paraphrasing includes:

- Replacing difficult vocabulary words or phrases with words the student understands

- Rewriting lengthy or complex sentences into simpler sentences, or combining simple sentences into more interesting, complex sentences

- Explaining concepts and abstract ideas from sentences or passages using more clear and concise wording

- Translating ideas and information into students' own words

Problems with underlying language-processing skills make paraphrasing especially difficult for students with language-based learning disabilities. Weaknesses, particularly at the semantic (word), syntactic (sentence), and discourse (paragraph) levels, minimize the ability to "play" with words. Limited vocabulary and ability to construct complex sentences make it difficult for students to come up with a "different way of saying things" in their own words.

Student Tips for Successful Paraphrasing

1. *Know how to choose and use a dictionary and a thesaurus:* Choose editions which are appropriate to your reading level and which have font styles and sizes that are easy to read. This includes dictionary and thesaurus features incorporated in word-processing software, which are often too advanced for students below grade ten.

2. *Understand the context of what you are paraphrasing:* Read the whole sentence or several sentences of the passage to have at least a general understanding of the context in which words

are being used. Make sure that the synonyms you use in your paraphrased version do not change the meaning of the passage.

3. *Use "semantic" paraphrasing:* Use a thesaurus and/or your own knowledge to replace words in the passage with accurate synonyms. Be sure to check the part of speech of the word you are replacing. How a synonym is used can change the meaning of the word or sentence.

4. *Use "syntactic" paraphrasing:* In addition to replacing key words, change the structure of the original sentences by either inverting the order of sentence parts, breaking them into shorter sentences, or combining simple sentences into compound and complex sentences.

5. *Rewrite the paraphrased version*: Combine the various changes noted above and rewrite the passage in your own words.

Simply asking students to restate something in their own words is not enough. It is important for teachers to model how to paraphrase and give numerous examples. Students need specific instruction in paraphrasing before they can independently apply this skill. The content material used in class lessons is a good source for examples. Teachers should review the portions of the textbook or supplemental reading material that will be used in class and pick out a few sentences or passages that are difficult to comprehend. Paraphrase these selections with the students in class. Discuss options for substituting synonyms and different sentence structures. Then when students read the material, encourage them to substitute the paraphrased versions so they can see how paraphrasing makes difficult reading more accessible.

PART II

Advanced Study Skills

CHAPTER 5

Textbook Skills

Students need several skills and strategies in order to understand the content of a textbook and place that understanding into long-term memory. Some students after reading — and re-reading — a chapter in a textbook are unable to remember the information. If these students simply "decode" while they read (translate the letters and syllables into words), they are technically reading but are not necessarily comprehending. In order to get the most from textbook reading, it is important to apply the following strategies:

- Pre-reading strategies to anticipate and give a purpose to reading

- Active reading strategies to read for meaning

- Organizational strategies to structure the information for easier recall

- Mastery strategies to move the information into long-term memory

Some students are able to develop these strategies on their own, but most require direct instruction. Textbook skills can be taught in elementary grades as soon as textbooks are introduced, but this instruction must continue through middle and high school as the complexity and volume of textbook material increases. Textbook skills are best taught in a content classroom so students can immediately see the value of applying these skills.

Identifying and Using Parts of a Textbook

First, students must learn how to recognize and use the basic parts of a textbook (e.g., the table of contents, index, glossary). They also must learn how to use the learning and study tools provided by textbooks (e.g., chapter maps and outlines, boldface headings).

Teachers should set aside time at the beginning of the year for "getting to know your textbook" and examine the different parts of the textbook with the class. Whenever the text is used in class, teachers should encourage students to use textbook aids. For example:

- Encourage students to use the table of contents or index when they have lost their place.

- As new words appear in the text, direct students to the glossary for definitions.

- When a new chapter or unit is introduced, direct students to the table of contents to see how the information is organized.

- Examine reading aids such as graphs, pictures, and summaries when introducing a new chapter.

Title and Copyright Pages

The title and copyright pages are often overlooked yet can yield some valuable information. To build student awareness about these pages, teachers can ask the following questions:

- What is the title, and what does it tell the reader about the main ideas in the book?

- Who is the author? What are his credentials? Is there more than one author?

- What does the copyright date tell us about how current the information is? (This is especially important when choosing books to use for research reports.)

Preface and Introduction

The preface and introduction provide valuable insight into the author's intention and the book's purpose. Some questions for teachers to ask:

- Why did the author write this book, and what did he want you to learn?

- What does the author want you to know before you read the book?

- Should the reader be aware of a particular bias on the author's part?

Table of Contents

The table of contents is actually an outline of the book. At a glance, it shows how the major topics in the book are organized, and how chapters and units relate to each other. Some questions for teachers to ask:

- How many chapters are there?

- Are the chapters grouped into units?

- What are the relationships between topics in chapters?

- How is each chapter organized? Does it start with an introduction? Is there a chapter summary at the end? Is the chapter divided into sections? Do these sections have headings or subheadings?

Give students practice using the table of contents to locate specific topics. Show students how a quick review of the table of contents can reveal major topics and provide valuable information on how to read the chapter by sections.

Graphic Aids
If pictures, graphs, charts, and other visual aids are included in the textbook, teachers should encourage students to use them as they read. Take time in class to read the captions beneath pictures and encourage students to find the section in the text that refers to the picture. Do not assume that students know how to read a graph, chart, or map. Provide practice exercises using these visual aids so students do not ignore them when they come across them in reading.

Study Aids
Most textbooks offer study aids such as chapter summaries, new vocabulary that is highlighted or italicized, lists or graphic organizers of key concepts, and review questions. Surprisingly, many students ignore these study aids or do not know how to use them. It is important for students to look them over before and after they read. Some questions for teachers to ask:

- Are the headings and subheadings different in some way from the rest of the text (boldface, a different size print)? If so, what does this tell you about how segments of the reading relate to each other?

- Can you turn the headings into questions?

- Are new vocabulary words italicized or in boldface? Are the definitions included?

- Are margin notes provided, or are key points highlighted in some way?

- Read the review questions at the end of each section or chapter. Where in the text can you find information to answer these questions?

- Is there an outline or a graphic organizer at the beginning or end of the chapter? What does this tell you about the major themes and main ideas in the chapter?

Glossary

Teach students how to use a glossary. Point out that it is an alphabetical list of important terminology used in the textbook. Students may not realize that the glossary is often easier to use than a dictionary because it gives the meaning of the terms as they are used in the book.

Index

The index is an alphabetical listing of topics and subtopics covered in a textbook. Many students are unaware that the index can help lead them to the location in the text where the answer to a homework or review question can be found. The index is particularly helpful when students are trying to find information for a research project.

When using the index, many students do not realize it is necessary to either limit or expand upon their topic in order to locate information. Suggestions in Chapter 2 for formulating a main idea can also help when formulating key words for an index search. Teachers should provide assignments using the index that give students practice finding page numbers for sample topics. For example, students can compete in teams the way they would on a scavenger hunt.

Pre-Reading Strategies

Pre-reading strategies enable students to read more actively and with a purpose. When students make use of pre-reading strategies, they are able to anticipate the ideas presented in a chapter and recognize how the ideas will be organized. Anticipating the main ideas provides a meaningful context during reading; it gives the student a "hook" on which to "hang" the details. Pre-reading strategies also build curiosity and interest by giving students the opportunity to think about the topic in relation to previously learned information or personal experience.

Surveying and Skimming

The first step in pre-reading is to survey the chapter. Students should spend a few minutes looking through the chapter and getting a general feel for what the chapter is about and how it is organized. This includes:

- Reading the title of the chapter to determine the over-all topic
- Noting how the chapter is listed in the table of contents
- Noting how many pages there are and if they are divided into sections
- Reviewing any graphs, pictures and their captions, or other visual aids

The next step is to skim over the chapter. Students should pay special attention to the introduction, titles and subtitles, words in italics or boldface print, margin notes or other notations, the conclusion, and any summaries or questions at the end of the chapter.

Identifying New Terminology

While pre-reading, students should identify any new or difficult vocabulary words, especially if the textbook highlights these words in some way. Definitions of these words should be written down before reading as a way to improve comprehension of the material.

Turning Headings into Questions

The best way to develop a purpose for reading is to formulate questions that can direct a search for answers while reading. Many textbooks supply questions at the end of the chapter that students can copy and refer to as they read. An excellent technique for generating questions is to turn the chapter headings and subheadings into questions. For example, the heading, "Applying Active Reading Strategies to Read for Meaning," on page 77 can be turned into the following question, "What are active reading strategies, and how do they help reading for meaning?" These heading questions will help students determine main ideas in the paragraphs.

Developing good questions is a skill that needs to be taught. Without some instruction in formulating useful questions, students will often generate simple "who," "where," and "when" questions that do little to help them read critically. Learning to frame "what," "why," and "how" questions will help them think about ideas and concepts as they read. Teachers should encourage students to develop a variety of questions that will identify factual material, as well as interpret and draw conclusions from main concepts.

Taking Time in Class to Preview

Teachers should be careful not to assume that students can apply surveying, skimming, and questioning skills. Providing time in class to preview before reading will encourage students to practice these skills and eventually to preview independently. Students usually want to do the minimum yet get the most from their schoolwork; they may initially see previewing as a superfluous task that is not worth the time. It is only after students have tried it and can see how their comprehension and memory are improved that they will accept it as a useful, and in the long run, time-saving skill.

When introducing a new chapter, teachers should encourage students to read the table of contents for the chapter and pre-read the headings and subheadings as a class. Before a reading assignment, give students a list of vocabulary words and have them locate the words in the passage and discuss the meanings. After providing a few minutes to pre-read the introduction, conclusion, and chapter summary, conduct a class discussion about what students think they will learn from their reading.

Finally, show students how to develop good pre-reading questions by providing examples. In the beginning of the year, hand out teacher-formulated questions. As the year progresses, instruct students to generate and critique each other's questions. Take advantage of opportunities to distinguish between good questions and those that are too specific or general. Many of the questions developed during pre-reading can be used later to anticipate and study for test questions. When returning a test or quiz, point out examples of the questions that were similar to those formulated during pre-reading.

Example 5A can be given to students to remind them how to preview before reading.

Example 5A

How to Preview a Textbook Chapter

Survey

1. Read the title to determine the topic of the chapter.

2. Look over the chapter in the table of contents to see how many sections it has and how each is organized.

3. Note how many pages are in the chapter and each section, and look over any graphs or pictures.

Pre-read

4. Skim the chapter and read the introduction, headings and sub-headings, words in italics, margin notes or other notations, and the conclusion to help anticipate what you will be reading.

5. Identify new vocabulary words. Find the definitions using the glossary or a dictionary and mark them in the book or on a piece of paper.

6. Turn headings and subheadings into questions. Be sure to include "why" and "what" questions to help identify main concepts. As you read, try to find answers to the questions.

Applying Active Reading Strategies to Read for Meaning

To read critically and commit information to memory, students must be active readers. They must search for answers to questions, organize main ideas and important details, and paraphrase information while reading. The best way to do this is to divide a chapter and read it in sections of several paragraphs to a few pages in length. As the students read each section, they should:

- Identify main ideas at the paragraph level

- Look for answers to the heading questions

- Highlight and make margin notes

What is the best way to teach highlighting? Most students, even those at the college level, do not highlight well. They either underline almost everything on the page or highlight only a few facts. Teachers should provide models of good highlighting and take time in class to practice these skills.

The first step in highlighting is to identify and highlight main idea phrases or topic sentences included in the paragraphs. (It is important to remember the topic sentence is not always the first sentence in the paragraph.) If the main ideas are not stated, and therefore must be inferred, they can be noted in the margin in the student's words. These become margin notes. The second step is to identify the most relevant and supportive details. It is helpful for students to highlight the main ideas with one color highlighter and the details with another color.

Students must already know how to recognize and formulate main ideas at the paragraph level in order to adequately highlight and make margin notes (see Chapter 2, "Recognizing and Formulating Main Ideas").

These skills can be practiced initially as a class. Students can take turns reading paragraphs out loud. Decide as a class which lines should be highlighted and where it would be helpful to write a margin note. Instruct students to use their previewing questions as guides. Point out that even something as long as a textbook can be broken down into manageable sections with main ideas.

If students are not allowed to write in the textbook, teachers should photocopy some of the pages so they can practice this skill. Also, a clear plastic sheet can be laid over the page. Students can use their highlighters and marking pens to practice, but when the sheet is removed, the textbook page remains clean.

Reflecting While Reading

Thinking about the ideas presented in a reading selection and expressing those ideas in one's own words are two skills that will enable students to read critically. As students become active readers and reflect on the material in their textbooks, they improve their critical thinking skills. Many students get excited about developing this ability. Teachers can reinforce critical reading skills by asking students to share their opinions about the points the author makes and by encouraging students to give critiques of the reading. Insist that students give specific examples from the reading to support their opinions.

At the end of every reading section, the questions formulated during pre-reading should be reviewed, and the information from the reading section used to formulate answers. This is another way to strengthen students' critical reading skills. Then teachers can ask the following general questions:

- How does this relate to what I have already learned in class and through reading?

- How does this relate to what I have learned in other classes?

- How does this relate to my own experience?

Organizational Strategies for Structuring Information

Creating Notes and Outlines
When we read multiple pages of text, it is easy to get "lost in the details." To help keep us on track, we can use the margin notes and the information we have highlighted to develop organizational tools such skeleton notes, outlines, and graphic organizers. These tools provide an organized "map" for finding our way through pages of information. They help us identify and structure the essential information so we can study it in an efficient, organized way. Also, as we actively sort through the reading to identify and paraphrase the essential information, we increase our opportunities for moving that information into our long-term memory.

To create skeleton notes or an outline, either the teacher or students can write on a separate piece of paper the textbook headings and subheadings, and the margin notes and highlights of the main ideas. These notes should be recorded into a two-column format (main ideas on the left, details on the right) or in a traditional outline format. A limited number of key details can also be included. When it is time to study for a test, these notes and outlines become study guides, eliminating the need to re-read the text.

Graphic Organizer of the Chapter
Before students begin a new text chapter, it is helpful for teachers to introduce a graphic organizer for the chapter. Start by taking all of the chapter headings, sections headings, and other bold print main ideas that are included in the chapter. Either skim through the chapter to locate them or check the table of contents which will sometimes list them. Arrange the headings at the top of the page similar to the top part of a flow chart. Use squares and circles to indicate different levels of main ideas. Once students begin reading and highlighting by paragraphs, they can add these main ideas under the appropriate heading on the flow chart (see Example 3G, a graphic organizer of Chapter 3, "Note-Taking"). While the teacher can ini-

tially create the graphic organizers for chapter study, students should ultimately learn to create these themselves.

As the class proceeds through the chapter, the teacher should stop every so often to ask students to identify where they are in terms of the overall picture of the chapter. This will help them step back from the details to see how the information they covered yesterday relates to what they are covering today. These graphic organizers are also helpful for parents to see at a glance what their children are learning during any given week. When the chapter is completed, the graphic organizer can be used to identify sections, or "chunks" of information that can be reviewed one unit at a time.

Creating Two-Column Vocabulary Study Guides

Students often have to learn new vocabulary from textbooks. Teachers should encourage students to use a different colored highlighter to underline new vocabulary and definitions that are imbedded in the text. At the end of the chapter, students can put the vocabulary words on the left side of a two-column page of notes. On the right side, they can copy the highlighted definitions or copy the definition from a glossary or dictionary. This two-column format makes it easy to study new vocabulary. Students can look at the words in the left column and cover the definitions on the right for self-quizzing.

Mastery Strategies for Long-Term Memory

Reviewing and Expressing Information After Reading

Simply reading a passage does not commit material to memory. Any review of reading material should include students' expression of the information in their own words. Even students who have organized and learned the information may not be able to adequately express their understanding in class or on a test if they have not first practiced expressing it in their own words. Strategies for reading with a purpose (formulating and answering questions, highlighting, reflecting, note-taking) will improve long-term memory and offer some opportunity for practice putting information into the students' own words. However, there are several additional tasks that can be done to improve study.

Summarizing

Using the suggestions presented in Chapter 4, "Summarizing and Paraphrasing," teachers can show students how to create a section or chapter summary with their highlighted main ideas and margin notes as an outline for the summary. If the chapter is long, several summaries can be written, one for each section of the chapter.

Modeling is a useful way to teach students how to generate summaries. Teachers should hand out a summary to go along with a reading when it is first assigned. After students read the passage, spend time in class discussing where each main idea in the summary originated in the passage. Next, students can write their own summaries. The teacher can provide a sample summary for comparison. Students can share and critique each other's summaries to see if they are complete. Textbooks often have summaries at the end of the chapter; use these for comparison as well.

Answering Questions

Questions provided by the textbook, or pre-reading questions generated by either the teacher or student, should be reviewed again once the chapter has been read. Students should use these questions for review and a clue as to what might be found on a chapter test. Instruct students to answer these as if they were essay questions on a test. They may be surprised to find that some of the real test questions will be similar to their own. Having already written about the topic, they will feel more comfortable when answering these questions during the actual test.

Review Within 24 Hours

Reviewing notes and studying material within 24 hours after reading significantly increases the effectiveness of the review and retention of the material. This is the best time to review because much of the information will still be in working and short-term memory and therefore more easily accessed. If students wait longer than 24 hours, they will essentially be starting over in the learning process. The same is true for studying information following lectures. Therefore, teachers should encourage students to review their notes either that same evening or the next day. Teachers can help develop a habit for immediate review by providing class time for reviewing notes or by assigning it for homework that night.

During this first review, students should organize and store all the notes, study questions, summaries, teacher handouts, and any other material that they will use to study later. This should be done on a daily and weekly basis (see Chapter 6, Summary of the Master Notebook System). The more thorough this initial review and the more organized the material, the easier and more effective studying will be for the test.

In Conclusion

Following the steps in this chapter for effective textbook use will not be an easy task, especially for students who are not used to spending the time to micro-unit a reading assignment. Learning how to use a textbook is a continuous process that takes place over several grades and is refined as students pass through high school and college. Teachers at each level can contribute to this process by providing class time to apply textbook study skills and by encouraging students to do so when they work independently.

CHAPTER 6

Study and Mastery: The Master Notebook System

The Landmark Master Notebook System is an ongoing system of organizing, studying, and mastering material. It includes three phases:

Phase I: Organizing Notebooks

Phase II: Studying

Phase III: Mastery

Chapter 1, "Organizational Skills," describes the steps for Phase I: setting up a working notebook, creating a reserve accordion file, and developing a reference section in the notebook. Chapter 6 will review strategies for Phase II and Phase III of the system (study and mastery). It is recommended that study strategies for Phase II (recording, editing, and reciting) be practiced on a daily basis, and mastery strategies for Phase III (expressing and reviewing the information in the student's own words) be practiced weekly.

Even if students understand what they read or hear in class, they do not necessarily commit the information to long-term memory.(see introduction, "Memory Issues and Study Skills"). In order to perform well on tests, participate in class discussions, and remember information for future classes, students must practice expressing this new information in their own words. By thinking about, questioning, reorganizing, writing, and talking about information in their own words, students will develop the ability and confidence to explain and prove what they have learned.

Phase II: Studying

In Chapter 3, "Note-Taking," a distinction was made between "note-taking" and "note-making." **Note-taking** involves learning and applying an organized format, such as two-column notes, to record information on paper from reading material or lectures. **Note-making** refers to active reading and listening strategies that help a student comprehend information and begin to place that comprehension into memory (see Chapter 5, Applying Active Reading Strategies to Read for Meaning). Phase II of the Master Notebook System emphasizes note-making; students are taught strategies to learn information from two-column notes that have been taken while reading or listening.

Phase II consists of a three-step study process: record, edit, and recite. It is an adaptation of the system for taking lecture notes developed at Cornell University.[2]

Record

The first step is to record notes using the two-column format (see Chapter 3, "Note-Taking"). It is essential that all the main ideas and key details are included in the notes. For notes from reading, the headings, sub-headings, and paragraph main ideas will be recorded in the left column, and the supporting details will be recorded in the right. Highlighted material and margin notes should also be included. It is sometimes difficult to determine the main ideas during a lecture. If this is the case, students should concentrate on recording the details in the right column during the lecture and formulating the main ideas in the left column later. While taking notes, students should leave plenty of room on the page to add information that might have been missed during the lecture.

Edit

After the information is recorded, the next step is to edit and revise the notes to be sure they are complete and easy to read. Editing steps include:

1. Check that all the main ideas are recorded in the left column, and be sure they are expressed completely and concisely.

2. Check that all the important details are recorded in the right column. If there is irrelevant information, cross it out.

3. Reduce wording to concise phrases, especially if the notes were initially taken in complete sentences. This will condense the notes and improve students' ability to take efficient notes.

4. Look at abbreviations to be sure they make sense. If necessary, write out the abbreviations into full words.

5. Add visual marks to make it easier to see how information in the notes is related. Draw horizontal lines across the page when the information supporting one main idea ends and another begins. Draw arrows to show connections between lines of notes. Add numbers to emphasize the order of details. Use a highlighter to accentuate key words or phrases.

[2]Pauk, Walter. 1962. *How to Study in College.* Boston: Houghton Mifflin.

6. Make sure all the note pages are numbered, dated, and in order.

Recite

Once the information is accurately recorded and edited, the notes are ready for students to recite. In this step, students cover the left column of the notes and try to remember the main ideas. They do this by reviewing the details to see what they have in common. Next, students cover the right column of the notes. They turn the main ideas into questions and try to remember the details as an answer to the main idea questions.

Editing and reciting should take place as soon as possible after initial notes have been taken, preferably within 24 hours. This will help transfer the information from basic working memory to long-term memory. If the notes were taken from a lecture, the best time to edit and recite is the few minutes between classes or at the end of the school day. If the notes are taken from reading, students should take a few minutes after the book is closed to edit and recite the information from their notes.

Teaching Suggestions for Recording, Editing, and Reciting

A natural place to introduce and practice Phase II strategies is during a review session in class. After a lecture, teachers should demonstrate on the board how to edit the notes and recite them. After modeling the skill, teachers should give students time following a lecture to practice editing their notes in class. Then the students can practice the reciting step by working in pairs. When they are comfortable with this process, they can practice both steps as a homework assignment. Once they can independently apply these strategies and begin to see how it is improving class discussion, homework, and test results, teachers can stop assigning it specifically for homework and suggest they continue to do it on their own. Periodically, as review, teachers should practice these skills together as a class to be sure students are continuing to be precise and thorough in their application of these skills.

Phase III: Mastery

Once students are routinely able to record, edit, and recite their notes, they are ready to learn mastery strategies.

Expressing the Information in Students' Own Words

Developing the ability to express information in students' own words is the first step toward mastery of the information. Thinking about the information in the notes and expressing those thoughts provides a way to prepare for tests, and an opportunity to learn a subject so well that students can offer original thoughts or observations based on reflection. Use the following steps with students to strengthen these skills:

1. Predict and write test questions based on the lecture notes and text readings. Answer them in writing as completely as possible. Check questions and answers with another student, and ask the teacher for clarification or assistance if you are confused or unsure about the information.

2. Whenever possible, draw diagrams, maps, or pictures to represent the information in a nonverbal way.

3. Create acronyms or other mnemonic devices to remember facts or lists of information (e.g., "HOMES" to remember the Great Lakes: Huron, Ontario, Michigan, Erie, and Superior).

4. Look for relationships and connections between ideas and write down the questions they raise, such as:

   • How does this relate to other things I have read or heard? (e.g. information from books, articles, handouts, or discussions)

   • How does this relate to what I am studying in other classes?

   • How does this relate to my own experience? (things I have seen or things that have happened to me)

5. Prepare flash cards for memorizing details (definitions, formulas, names, and dates) and quiz yourself throughout the week. Put the vocabulary word or question on one side of the card and the definition or answer on the other side. Mark a card each time you miss the answer. When you have several marks, set the card aside for special attention. When you correctly identify a card several times, remove it from the pile-you have learned it! Learn the cards "backwards and forwards." Identify them from the front or from the back.

6. Write a summary of the information that includes all the main points from your notes (see Chapter 4, "Summarizing and Paraphrasing"). Try to identify a central theme that ties all the

main points together, and use transitional words or phrases to show how ideas are related.

Students can use the blank, reverse side of the previous page of notes (called a "mastery page") as a work area for the first four tasks and for the summary if there is room.

Teachers should encourage students to apply these mastery strategies on a daily basis so they are dealing with manageable amounts of information. If students wait until the end of a unit of study, they will be overwhelmed by the amount of information.

Reviewing the Information

The final step in the mastery phase is a weekly review. Set aside one day a week for each subject. On this day, students should review the original notes and the accompanying summaries, flash cards, and other mastery strategies noted above. For example, on Mondays, in addition to the regularly assigned homework, students should review English. History is reviewed on Tuesday, science on Wednesday, and so forth. This keeps the information active in long-term memory so that when it is time to study for a test, it does not have to be re-learned.

Once a week, students should do the following things:

1. Recite from the beginning all of the notes in the working notebook. As students add new notes, the spiraling back over previous notes will keep the information fresh.

2. Go through notes and other papers to determine what can be removed from the working notebook and put in the reserve accordion file. Make a coversheet for the packet that includes the dates the notes were taken, a topical outline, and a summary, as explained in Chapter 1, "Organizational Skills."

3. Review test questions, flash cards, acronyms, and diagrams that were developed during the study phase. Refine and elaborate answers. Think again about the topics covered. Make a note of new ideas or questions to bring up in class.

Teaching Strategies

The mastery phase can be introduced as part of a periodic review of material. Teachers should introduce the students to the steps and then demonstrate them in class. It is especially important to model the use of the mastery page in the notebook. After practicing the skill in class, assign students to do the same for homework. Periodically review the mastery strategies as a class activity so students can continue to refine their application of these skills. It is important that at each step of the process, students understand why these strategies will improve long-term memory of material. This understanding will encourage students to apply these strategies independently.

Summary of the Master Notebook System

Strategies for all three phases of the Master Notebook System should be practiced and applied throughout the school year.

On a daily basis, students should:

1. Check that they have all the necessary materials and supplies in their notebooks.

2. Record information from lectures and reading using a two-column note-taking format.

3. Edit and recite notes, preferably within 24 hours.

On a weekly basis, students should:

1. Sort through their working notebook and pull out notes, assignments, and returned tests. At the end of a unit of study, they should create a cover sheet and move the packet into the reserve accordion file.

2. Apply strategies for expressing the information in their own words.

3. Review notes, summaries, and flash cards to the point of mastery.

Instruction in the Master Notebook System, especially the organization of notebooks, should begin as early as fourth grade. Study and mastery strategies should be introduced at the beginning of middle school, but students will continue to need instruction and modeling in these strategies during high school before they can independently apply all phases of the system. The following chart suggests the level at which students may reach independence with each phase of the system.

	Phase I Organize	Phase II Study	Phase III Mastery
Upper Elementary	with help	introduce	introduce
Middle School	with help	with help	introduce
High School	independent	with help	with help
College	independent	independent	independent

CHAPTER 7

Test Preparation and Test-Taking Skills

For some students, taking a test is the most dreaded part of the school experience. In order to do well on a test, students must understand the questions, organize the answers, and produce a well-written response within a limited time period. All this must be done under the pressure of knowing that performance on the test may significantly affect the grade for a course.

Test performance is not necessarily related to how much time students study. Some students spend a lot of time trying to study, but do poorly because they do not have good test preparation and test-taking skills. They are willing to study but do not know how to do so effectively. Others may have adequately mastered the material but are afraid and disorganized during the test, and therefore do not do as well as they could. Instruction and practice with test-taking skills can result in better test preparation, improved test performance, and reduced test anxiety.

Teaching Test Preparation

Test preparation begins on the first day of class and continues throughout the semester. If students apply good textbook skills (see Chapter 5) and keep Master Notebooks (see Chapter 1 and Chapter 6), they are preparing for tests by regularly reviewing and expressing in their own words the information they learn from lectures, reading assignments, and class discussions. Editing and reciting notes, creating summaries, and formulating and answering study questions on a consistent basis alleviate the need to "cram" before a test. When students wait until the night before a test, they must try to re-learn weeks of information all at once. In addition, the anxiety created by last minute studying may erode their confidence and performance during the test. Reviewing material within 24 hours after it is presented significantly increases the chances it will be remembered in long-term memory.

Class Review

A good way to demonstrate test preparation skills is through class review. Many teachers announce a test date and give the class a day of review before the test. Although this review time is helpful, it is more effective to conduct frequent, short class reviews. Instead of reviewing everything in one day, teachers should spend a little time each day reviewing portions of the material. This will set an example for how test information can be studied in sections. Also, instead of telling students what they should study for a test, teachers should encourage students as a class to determine what they think they will need to know.

After students have taken notes from a lecture or textbook, teachers should demonstrate how to edit the notes into succinct main ideas and key details. Then, as a class, recite the notes. Give students class time to practice editing and reciting independently and eventually assign these skills for homework. The same procedure should be followed for creating summaries and developing study questions. It is important that at each step of the process students understand why they are applying these strategies so they develop an awareness of how they learn.

Sometimes the most effective time for review is after a test has been taken and graded. Teachers should provide class time to analyze the questions and discuss what should have been studied. Students can learn from their mistakes as they go back over notes, summaries, and study questions to correct their answers.

Identifying Topics to be Studied

In addition to regularly practicing editing, reciting, and mastery skills, there are several steps students can follow to prepare a week or two before a test. They can begin by determining what topics will be covered on the test and organizing this information into a list of main ideas. These lists should be compatible with the study packets they have stored in their reserve accordion file (see Chapter 1). This list should enable them to microunit the material and study it one section at a time.

After teachers announce a test date, work as a class to generate a main idea list. Ask the students to think about how much emphasis was placed on each topic as the unit was taught, and use that information to determine what the test will include. In some classes, the teachers may need to provide this list for students until the students become adept at formulating it themselves. Initially, students can work in pairs to determine the topics for the test. Eventually this task can be given as a homework assignment.

Determining What Kind of Questions will be on the Test

There is a real advantage to knowing what types of questions will be on the test. Will it be all objective and short-answer questions, an essay test, or a combination of both? The types of questions that will appear on the test should determine how students prepare for a test and what type of information they study.

Objective test questions (true/false, multiple choice, matching, fill-in-the-blank) usually require students to recognize or recall factual information, details from the right columns of their notes, and vocabulary terms. Covering the detail columns of notes and using the main ideas to quiz for these details is a good way to study this type of information. As a class activity, teachers should encourage students to search their notes for terms or important details to put on flash cards. Students can quiz each other using these cards, or they can have someone at home help them.

Essay questions, on the other hand, usually test for main ideas and concepts and require answers that reflect critical thinking. Writing summaries and answering practice essay questions throughout the semester will prepare students for these test questions. Remind students that knowing the answer is sometimes not enough; they have to practice expressing the information in order to perform well on essay tests.

Beginning in the elementary grades, teachers should instruct students in the different types of test questions. Some students, for example, do not know how to answer matching or true/false questions. Be sure they know how to approach these and other types of questions so they can be judged on their knowledge of answers rather than their ability to comprehend the question or produce the correct type of answer.

Two essay questions about the same topic can require very different answers depending on how the question is phrased. Many students answer essay questions by writing everything they know about the topic and lose points because they do not address the specifics of the question. Words such as "compare," "contrast," "define," "discuss," "relate," "illustrate," "evaluate," and "review" have subtle differences in meaning. A review of these terms will improve students' ability to provide accurate answers to essay questions.

Planning Study Time

Chapter 1, "Organizational Skills," emphasizes the importance of teaching students how to use calendars and other tools to budget their time. Teachers should use time-planning strategies to create a study schedule before a test. Once a test date is announced, note it on the large classroom calendar recommended in Chapter 1. Remind students to write the date in their personal calendars. As a class, determine how many days are left before the test and plan time each day for studying. Show students how to plan some weekend time for studying while at the same time being realistic about other recreational and personal time commitments.

After the class determines a plan for studying, remind students each night what they should cover and, if possible, assign this as part of their homework. This approach will model organized test preparation and eventually demonstrate that it is easier and more effective to study a little bit every night than it is to try to review everything the night before. Using a calendar to plan study time is extremely useful when several tests from different classes are scheduled for the same day or week. Without some help on how to devise a plan of attack for studying different subject areas, some students may over-study one subject and neglect others.

Example 7A reviews the steps for "How to Prepare for a Test," and can be given to students to keep in their reference notebooks.

Forming Study Groups

Joining together in study groups during class or at home is an underused study technique that can be quite helpful. However, most students do not know how to organize an effective study group and need to be given a format that will make the time productive.

Three to five students is a good number for a study group, although two students can also be effective study partners. The group should begin to meet as soon as the test is announced. During the first meeting, students should determine what topics will be covered on the test. These topics should be divided between the number of students in the group. Each member then prepares ten to fifteen study questions that cover both the main ideas and details for their topic. Students ask questions of each other and state the answers in complete sentences. The student asking the question should prepare a written answer that can be handed out to the other students and used as a reference for any information the other students may forget.

Participation in this type of study process provides several modalities for reviewing information. In addition to reading and writing in preparation for the study group, the students also have a chance to listen to the answers given by others and then talk about them.

As a way of modeling this interaction, study groups can be formed by the teacher and meet during class time. Ask groups to create possible test questions and then answer them. Teachers should include some of the student-prepared questions on the test as a way to reward this type of studying.

Example 7A

How to Prepare for a Test

Throughout the Semester:

1. Highlight, take notes, and review all assigned reading.

2. Edit and review notes from reading and lectures within 24 hours.

3. On a weekly basis, write summaries and answer study questions from each unit of material.

4. On a regular basis, organize notes, handouts, summaries, etc., into packets and store them in the reserve accordion file.

A Week or Two Before the Test:

1. Form an outline of all the main topics.

2. Use a calendar to plan your study time. Study the information in sections and spread it out over several days.

3. Form a study group and meet at least three times.

4. Prepare for essay questions by predicting questions and writing out answers.

5. Prepare for objective questions by making and studying flash cards.

Teaching Test-Taking

Success on tests should reflect how well students have learned the material. Unfortunately, students who know the material may lose points on a test because they have not learned test-taking strategies. Instruction on how to begin a test, how to plan time during the test, and how to answer different types of test questions (especially essay questions), results in test grades that are a more accurate reflection of what the students have learned.

How to Approach a Test

When students receive a test, they should first skim the test from beginning to end to determine what kinds of questions it includes and how they are arranged. They should also note the scoring criteria. Are some questions worth more points than others? How much of the score is based on essay answers? If students do not plan how they will proceed through the test, they may spend too much time on the first questions (which may not be worth many points) and not have enough time for essay questions at the end.

Teach students to develop a plan for how much time to spend on each section of a timed test. This plan should be based on how much each question is worth and how time-consuming it will be to answer. Simply suggesting that students plan wisely is not enough. They need to practice this in class or they will fall back on old habits during the test. Mock test formats can be used in class to practice (see Example 7B).

Encourage students to go through the test and complete all questions that they are confident they can answer in a reasonable amount of time. When they come to a difficult question, they should circle it and move on. If there is time at the end of test, they can go back and try to answer these questions. Make sure they remember to circle unanswered questions so they can locate them quickly and use any extra time to work on the answer.

It is important to read directions carefully and underline key words or instructions. Points are often lost on tests because students have not followed directions. For example, true/false questions sometimes require students to rewrite the answer to make it true if they think the answer is false. If they do not read the directions carefully, they may neglect to do this. Sometimes misreading or leaving out a simple word can change how a question is answered. A multiple-choice question may ask students to choose the best answer, but if they haven't noted the word "best," they may choose the first correct answer, even though it is not the best.

Example 7B

Test-Taking Strategy Worksheet

You have one hour to finish a test. The test contains the following types of questions:

—10 true/false questions worth 2 points each

—10 matching questions worth 2 points each

— 4 fill-in-the-blank questions worth 5 points each

— 2 essay questions worth 20 points each

You should give yourself the following time to complete these portions of the test:

    1. To skim the test _____

    2. True/false _____

    3. Matching _____

    4. Fill-in-the-blank _____

    5. First essay question _____

    6. Second essay question _____

    7. Extra time to review answers and proofread _____

Example 7C lists five steps for "How to Take a Test." It can be kept in the reference section of students' working notebooks.

Example 7C

How to Take a Test

1. Skim over the test to determine what types of questions it contains and how much they are worth.

2. Plan how much time to spend on each section. Stick to the plan!

3. Answer the questions you know in each section and circle the ones about which you are unsure. If there is time at the end of the test, go back and try the circled ones again. Do not waste time on answers you do not know.

4. Re-read directions and underline key words. Be sure to follow exact directions.

5. Leave time to review your answers at the end of the test.

Answering Essay Questions

Essay questions, which can account for a large portion of the score of a test, often pose the biggest challenge to students. For example, students often neglect to think through and organize the answer prior to writing their response to an essay question. Teachers should encourage students to follow these four steps when encountering an essay question.

1. **Analyze the Question:** Carefully read the question **twice** to be clear about what it is asking. Underline key words and divide the question into sections if it has several parts.

2. **Organize the Answer Before Writing:** Use an informal outline or list of ideas on a scratch piece of paper or in the margin to list the essential points you want to include. These notes are useful because they can help you remember all of your ideas and answer all parts of the question. This informal outline can also be used to help sequence the ideas in your answer.

3. **Write in a Clear, Orderly Style:** Begin the answer by stating exactly what you intend to say in your answer. Restating the

question in some way will do this. Next, develop the ideas in your informal outline by turning each into a structured paragraph that states the point and includes supporting details or examples. Try to provide evidence to back up any statements or positions you take. Refer to the question and informal outline several times to avoid straying from the topic. Some students have the mistaken notion that the more they write, the better their answer will be. In fact, teachers frequently give more credit to a shorter answer if it is concise and well organized.

4. **Proofread the Answer:** Take the time to re-read the answer for basic composition errors (punctuation, capitalization, sentence structure), and be sure your answer is complete. Always write your answers in pencil so you can make changes!

Teachers should give students practice with these steps by requiring them to answer sample essay questions in class and for homework. With enough practice, students will internalize the process and apply it automatically in a test situation. Example 7D can be distributed to students and used during a test to remind them of the steps they should follow. This reminder may help reduce some of the anxiety students often experience when they are confronted with essay questions.

Example 7D

How to Answer an Essay Question

1. Read the question twice.

2. Underline key words. Note how many parts there are to the question.

3. In the margin or on a scratch piece of paper, jot down and categorize key points for the answer.

4. Re-state the question in an introductory sentence.

5. Write the answer following your informal outline. Use paragraphs and be concise. Give examples and supporting evidence when possible.

6. Proofread for punctuation, capitalization, and sentence structure. Be sure you answered the question completely.

Test Anxiety

Sometimes test anxiety can be so severe that, even when students are prepared, they forget the answer. Failure in previous test situations can undermine the confidence students develop from their newly learned test-taking strategies. As noted in the introduction, providing opportunities for success in test-taking situations can help overcome this anxiety.

Teachers should design the first tests and quizzes of the year to be short and simple. It is better to have students take a number of short tests rather than one long one so they have several opportunities to practice test-taking skills. Give some open-book tests where students can use their notes and other prepared study guides during the test. This will eliminate the fear of "going blank" that worries some students. Open-book tests also provide a good opportunity to demonstrate the importance of keeping a complete and organized notebook. Similarly, allow students to use a one-page study sheet while they are taking a test. As students begin to feel successful in test-taking situations, they will be less anxious about taking tests in the future.

CHAPTER 8

Research and Report-Writing

High school teachers and college instructors are sometimes surprised when students who usually do well in their classes have difficulty writing good research reports. This is not surprising, however, given the many steps involved in producing a research report. To prepare students for this task, teachers must introduce report-writing skills as early as the fourth grade and continue instruction through high school. Content classroom teachers and skill teachers alike have a responsibility to teach these important skills.

Research and report-writing skills can be grouped into the following categories:

1. Selecting, narrowing, and brainstorming a topic

2. Using the library, the World Wide Web, and other sources of information

3. Organizing information to create topical and final outlines

4. Producing first and final drafts

5. Constructing a bibliography and assembling footnote information

Applying Study Skills to Research and Report-Writing

Students will produce better papers if they have already learned good organizational, note-taking, summarizing, and textbook skills as follows:

Organizational Skills: Students need organizational skills in order to divide a research project into manageable steps and to plan a schedule for completing each step. They also need these skills in order to keep track of note cards and bibliography information.

Main Idea and Note-Taking Skills: In order to gather relevant information from sources, students need the ability to distinguish between main ideas and details, and the ability to practice good note-taking skills. Note-taking skills enable students to group information into main ideas that can be used to create a topical outline necessary to writing a first draft.

Summarizing Skills: Summarizing and paraphrasing skills are key to students successfully locating information from sources and translating it into their own words. If students have learned how to write succinct summaries, they will be better able to create note cards from lengthy passages in books. These skills are also essential to avoid plagiarism.

Textbook Skills: Recognizing and knowing how to use different parts of a book (table of contents, index, glossary, and chapter summaries) helps students locate relevant information. Pre-reading skills enable students to quickly review sources to determine if the information is useful. Highlighting, margin note-taking, and creating two-column notes from text are necessary skills for efficient and accurate collection of information.

Assigning Research and Report Projects

Micro-Unit and Structure the Project
When assigning a research project, teachers should hand out a list of steps similar to the one in Example 8A. Teach one step at a time, making sure students understand how the steps relate to each other. Assign due dates for each of the following steps:

1. A final topic that has been narrowed and brainstormed

2. A topical outline

3. Note cards

4. A preliminary bibliography

5. A final outline

6. A first draft

7. The final report

Give a grade for each step of the project that will be averaged into the final grade. This will reinforce that the process for completing a good research report is just as important as the finished product. It will also provide structure for those students who do not plan well and who would otherwise end up doing all the work at once.

Budget Enough Time to Complete the Project
Teachers should plan due dates that allow enough time to teach the skill and sufficient time for students to implement the step. For example, be sure to provide at least a few days for choosing and narrowing a topic.

Teachers should keep in mind that the goal for a research project should be to learn the strategies and process for researching and reporting, not sim-

Example 8A

Steps to Prepare a Research Report

1. Choose and narrow a topic. Read an encyclopedia entry or short article to familiarize yourself with the topic. This will help narrow the topic.

2. Brainstorm key words and subtopics. Use them to research books and other resources on your topic.

3. Formulate questions to help guide your search for information.

4. Organize the sub-topics into a topical outline.

5. Locate and narrow your final sources: use the library card catalogue, guides to periodical literature, encyclopedias and other references, primary resources, and information from the World Wide Web. Expand your sources to include more than just books.

6. Read and collect information from all your sources.

   —Pre-read and identify which information is relevant.

   —Take notes on index cards.

   —Paraphrase in your own words, or note direct quotes with quotation marks.

   —Mark page numbers and names of sources on each note card so you can properly footnote.

7. Make bibliography cards of all the sources you have used.

8. Develop a detailed outline before writing.

9. Write a first draft:

   —Write information from your note cards and outline into paragraphs with clear main ideas.

   —Organize your paper into sections and label each with a heading.

   —Include an introduction and conclusion.

   —Formulate your final title.

   —Use footnotes to document where you found your information.

10. Write the final draft of your report: rewrite, delete, add, change the order, etc. to improve your paper. Proofread for consistent tense, spelling, capitalization, and punctuation.

11. Construct a final bibliography from your bibliography cards.

---

ply writing a good report. Require students to hand in note cards, outlines, and first drafts. Plan class time to go over this material as the project progresses. It is much better for students to take a longer time completing one good report than to rush to complete two reports.

Provide Clear, Organized Directions

Provide clear directions for each step of the research process. Save outlines, note cards, first drafts, and final papers from previous classes and make them available as models. Include examples of both well-prepared and weak reports so students can make comparisons. It is also helpful to provide a "directions packet" for students. It can include the following guidelines:

1. A cover sheet stating general report requirements (length, number of sources, etc.)

2. A planning calendar with due dates

3. A list of steps detailing each stage of the report

4. Requirements for and samples of note cards, footnotes, and bibliography

5. Requirements and suggestions for first and final drafts

6. A summary of the grading criteria

The amount of direction included in this packet is up to the teacher. Require students to bring the directions packet to class and refer to it every time a new step is introduced. Even when students are capable of completing papers independently, hand out a packet to remind them of the expectations.